MASTER DEALING WITH PSYCHOPATHS, SOCIOPATHS AND NARCISSISTS

The Ultimate Handbook for the Empath

Zane Alexander

Publication and Use Disclaimer

The information, advice, and suggestions in this book are distributed on an 'as is' basis, without warranty. While every precaution has been taken in the preparation of this book, neither the author nor the publisher shall have any liability to any person or entity with respect to any loss or damage alleged to be caused directly or indirectly using the ideas, opinions, and suggestions contained in this book. The advice and contents of this book may not be suitable for your situation. This book contains responsible and helpful advice about dealing with psychopathic and sociopathic individuals and should be considered as reference work only, not intended as a substitute for professional advice. The reader is responsible for his or her own actions. Any perceived slight of any individual, field, or organization is purely unintentional. This book does not replace advice from accredited professionals and/or mental health and/or counseling and/or professional psychological therapy that might be required in the aftermath and/or current association and/or relationships with psychopaths, sociopaths, and narcissists. It should be clear to you that by law we make no guarantees that you will achieve any results from the ideas presented in this book, and we offer no professional legal, medical, psychological, or financial advice.

Never be manipulated again.

– Zane Alexander

Table of Contents

A Note from the Author

This guide began in July 2015, as a result of shocking, personal experiences. It has been a research and writing effort of over two years, with me researching poignant topics for us empaths, then adding a new section every couple of months. My goal at the time was quality over quantity, with absolutely no fluff. This handbook was finally completed in 2018.

I want to thank everyone who bought the original, shorter version on Amazon, and everyone who took a leap of faith on an unknown author with real-world experience. I really appreciate this.

I will continue to write on my future blog at **Sociopath-Free.com**, providing tips, tools, and resources to live a life free from manipulation.

If you want top-notch articles delivered to you, please sign up at **SociopathFree.com/Signup**

Sincerely,

Zane Alexander
Formerly known as Transcendence

P.S. If you signed up to my mailing list before July 2017, I sincerely apologize for not notifying you of the new chapters of the book. This was due to a technical glitch in my mailing system. To make sure I have you on my future notification list, please sign up to the mailing list above to have my newest articles, courses, and all new information delivered right to your inbox.

Why I Wrote This Guide and Why You Should Read It

Like many people who have had encounters with a psychopathic or sociopathic individual, I am a once-naive empath who encountered them in various avenues of my life – heart broken, illusions stripped away, career path shattered, and a result of radical transformation. Somewhere in that abyss of self-searching darkness, I was finally able to put the puzzle together by an inkling of spiritual insight and wisdom. Like the candlelight glimmer of a hunch in a cave of blackness and broken fragments, I followed that intuitive light, as well as relied on our common human will, to rebound, rebuild, and regenerate.

After one year of obsessive reading and research, my paradigm of thinking shifted 180 degrees. My studies opened up a world I never imagined could exist. It felt like waking up with a different pair of eyes. Now, rather than approach the future fearfully, I am able to approach it practically.

For personal reference, I began summarizing everything useful I found on the topic, gathering my collection of reading materials from many different schools of thought – from the scientific, to the practical, to the spiritual and esoteric. The original intent was to use my new-found knowledge to form a long-term 'play book' of how to deal practically with real-life situations and people. This idea developed into creating an easy-to-reference guide and cheat sheet with a level of practicality and depth for everyday use.

Then I got thinking: how many empaths like me are out there who can benefit from something like this? How many

people will appreciate a shortened guide that is well organized, easy to understand, and easy to review?

Hence, my goals for the guide are to:

1. **Have an effective reminder to reference and read again
   and again, especially at moments when risking a fall into the internal battle of controlling our 'niceness' to the
   undeserving.**
2. **Thoroughly analyze and summarize the modus op-
   erandi of this type of being, so that the empath can
   have a lifetime reference for counter-methods of operation.**

Many times, the works of first-hand encounters with sociopaths, narcissists, and psychopaths read with too much emotion to serve as a practical guide. Although the emotional
fallout is no doubt justified, and its expression may be helpful for readers to explore and process their own emotions
after personal experiences with toxic and disordered individuals, the end work can be overly weighted toward angry
or bitter feelings, rather than positive actions. Every effort
has been made to ensure the contents here are focused on
providing the utmost practicality and usefulness to the reader.

I am not a psychiatrist or psychologist, nor do I have a PhD.
My interest is not in contributing to scientific research or
clinical tests. This work is intended as a reality-based resource for myself and others who can benefit from such input on a day-to-day level. My priority is a concise summary
focused on delivering value, substance and results, and the
rules of engagement for an empath. I hope it speaks to you.

In the creation of this guide, I was inspired by reading several other authors. I found myself sprouting seeds of an idea

while reading existing works in the niche, with those little seeds blossoming into newer, bigger concepts and solutions in my mind. In situations where another author first came up with a thought, concept, or idea, I cited and gave credit to the original source. Hence, this is a book built on my own experiences and advice, mixed with my interpretation of already established works in the niche. While most authors focus on the psychopath in specific settings, such as romance or the workplace, the goal here is to consolidate everything into one handy guide to deal with psychopaths, sociopaths, and narcissists in the game of life.

Lastly, let's define what an empath is – what is an empath? It's a very broad term that ranges from the capacity to empathize with another, to emotionally sensitive beings with the gift of intuiting and feeling others' emotions, as if they were their own. I am aware there are different levels and magnitudes of sensitivity, morality, and conscience. For the purpose of this guide though, I am defining an empath rather simply as anyone who possesses genuine empathy for another human being ... along with a conscience and the ability to love.

Please also note that I have included a fast and easy reference for NCEA (No Contact Ever Again) triggers on the following pages to serve as a practical, useful tool. Review this regularly for long-term results, as this is a necessary habit change for us empaths.

With much love and strength

Zane Alexander

Formerly known as Transcendence

A Key Reminder of the NCEA (No Contact Ever Again) Social Rule

To become winners in the long term, the most useful gift we can gather from experiences with psychopaths, sociopaths and narcissists is never letting lessons go to waste.

Most of you already know the world isn't all pink bubbles and sunshine. There are dark corners we must guard and fortify ourselves against. Ultimately, fleeing from the truth won't help. This reality is challenging, but it's necessary to accept it for self-protection, ammunition, and ultimately self-growth.

There are four primary challenges facing the empath as he or she learns to erect boundaries, uncover the wolves in sheep's clothing, and properly direct their naturally kind natures:

1. **The cognitive dissonance between manufactured appearance and inner reality.** Despite what we may have witnessed, experienced, or intuitively sensed, the outer presentations of the psychopath can be blindingly convincing.

2. **A battle of self-control to overcome our own inherent niceness.** We must learn to control and regulate our niceness to those who have no other motives than to exploit and harm.

3. **The myth that love conquers all.** The most empathetic among us are capable of deep, unconditional, universal love. However, we have to drill it home that there are situations and people to which this wonderful and amaz-

ing gift absolutely cannot apply. Paradoxically, giving such people those powerful energies will only harm you and your amazing potential for goodness. Staying away strengthens you, your capability, and the positive things you can ultimately do for those you care about, the world, and humanity.

4. **The temptation for adventure, excitement, and life experiences.** Many of us have an adventurous spirit and thirst for rich life experiences, wishing to experience everything life offers – whether it's extreme emotional experiences, different cultures, socio-economic circles, and so on. However, we must differentiate between what choices reflect a healthy excitement and what can be dangerous. We must have the intelligence and healthy suspicion to probe and research independently, along with the wisdom to judge and shut out unnecessary danger, which tends to come at a high cost. If all other potentially amazing life experiences you could experience in the future are robbed by one incident or person, that most definitely isn't worth it.

There will be times when you are temporarily overcome by the following in dealings with a shadowy individual:

- Emotions of pity, sympathy, compassion, or kindness.

- Warm and uplifting thoughts toward your fellow compatriots.

- The all-too-common empath's wish for happy endings.

- The painful desire for contact and closure.

- Confusion and second thoughts due to the giant disconnect between what is seen on the surface – the nice words; the authentic, sincere, altruistic, and kind persona; an in-demand, sexy, popular image – and the cruel, harmful, demeaning, malicious actions inflicted on others.

- Manufactured desperation, over-dependence, and other addictive behavior.

When those times happen, please read the points below over and over again for a dose of reality and clarity.

These feelings are part of a world view that must be deprogrammed and shifted for your long-term happiness and sanity. To help with this process, try reading through and contemplating the following five points:

1. **Thoroughly differentiate between words and actions. Mentally flag all obvious disconnects. Award trust only when it is earned.** Adopt the following three layers of observation before you give your trust away:
   - **Words – Don't trust them.** Words are very cheap. Golden promises are meaningless unless backed up by evidence of integrity. Kind, noble, and saintly semantics are uttered by everyday manipulators, so they can seem like one of the good guys. These characters even give moral-sounding advice that they themselves never abide by.

   - **Actions – A better predictor of character.** Place more trust in those whose words and actions align. If there is a disconnect between words and actions, notice this as a red flag. Do not ignore it, or you will regret it. An anonymous quote phrases it best: "When things don't add up, it's because the truth was not included in the equation."

- **The Little Moments – The best predictor of character.** These are the little things uttered, the little things done or not done; seemingly inconsequential, real, live, accidental, and unplanned moments. In those situations, what does the person do or say? How do they treat those who can do nothing for them, especially when they think no one's watching? These are the red flags that hold the secrets to the truth. These tiny behaviors reveal the true personality and motives of the person in question. Why? Because they are accidental and real, not pre-planned to impress or calculated for an agenda. No one can keep up pretense 24/7 in all situations.

2. **Not all people are inherently good or instinctively know right from wrong.** There are people in the world who are secretly filled with envy, who have no redeeming motives, who exist only to hurt others for self-satisfaction and exploitation. **Such people will never change.** You will never find a soft spot within them, and there is nothing you can do to persuade them to behave differently.

3. **Appearances are deceiving.** Most psychopaths are not creepy at first sight. Appearances are usually everything to a psychopath. Whether it's an innocent face, saintly words, or a flawless image of prestigious brand names, flashy cars, and massive social popularity – the presentation is nothing but an illusion. Learn to probe beneath that pretty show. Differentiate between the surface mirage and the character and substance that lies beneath.

"The women, they underestimate me for ... I look like an ordinary person. That was their downfall. My appearance was different from what I really was."

– Gary Ridgway (Serial Killer)

4. **Not all people have a capacity to love and emotionally connect with other human beings.** Research suggests that certain individuals, through a combination of genetic and environmental factors, have a psychological inability to love and empathize. Such individuals see empathy as a flaw, and compassion as weakness – vulnerable points they will exploit for their own purposes, without caring in the slightest how their actions affect you. Associating with them using your normal demeanor can be draining and ineffective at best, and dangerous at worst. It's best to direct your intrinsic gifts of love, compassion, and kindness to those who have passed the test of time and to learn to shield yourself against toxic people with a steel, unrelenting, rock-solid, impenetrable wall that shuts them out forever.

5. **Love does not conquer all – not with a psychopath.** The stark reality is that some people are not capable of understanding or being influenced by love or affection. Investing energies of affection in them will only destroy and weaken you, perhaps to a point of no return. You are too important and valuable to be drained by a human black hole. The stronger you are, the more you can give to the world and those you care about. The weaker you become, the less you can do for the world and for those you care about.

Protecting yourself in this rather cold manner may seem paradoxical. But if you are a true empath with good intentions, and if you wish to be unselfish, the best thing you can do for others (and for humanity in general) is strengthening yourself for your own self-preservation. You do that by shutting out the toxic people who weaken and drain you. This action opens up your time, heart, and energy to give to those who truly matter. Think about all the love you can give, all the people you can touch, and all the potential you can contribute to help others over a longer-term period. Is it really worth sacrificing all your positive potentials, for one twisted and morally bankrupt individual, who contributes nothing to the world at all?

To conclude this section, we can observe that psychopaths, sociopaths, and narcissists are poor investments for intelligent, wise people.

They offer:

- No real love or affection.

- No loyalty or fidelity.

- Abandonment if you become a burden, even at the pivotal times in life when it really matters.

- The possibility of being good in bed. However, this one potentially positive factor is outweighed by the likelihood of carrying sexually transmitted diseases from massive levels of philandering. You can't trust their actions or what they say. They could easily put your health at risk at any time.

- The likelihood, in relationships, of living off of you, giving no financial contribution at all. This kind of behavior can be a clear red flag. Honorable men or women of substance and character have too much pride and self-reliance to drain resources without contributing in today's day and age.

Working through these points with increased clarity, you begin to see the world as it truly is, and you may even see yourself as you truly are. Good intentions do not guarantee that the one we are projecting them to is capable of returning them.

"Letting go of toxic people in your life is a big step in loving yourself."

– Unknown

Chapter 1
The 80/20 Basics

Forget about all the social rules you thought you knew.

The stark reality is that 4% of the population wears a socially acceptable mask which hides a world view and code of conduct we can never begin to understand.[1]

When you are confronted with harmful, confusing, mind-bogglingly destructive actions, it seems impossible to do anything but ask incredulously, *"What is wrong with those people?!"* These people are an insidious force of dark energy, felt but unseen. They are a completely alien species.

Most of us never knew that this type of person existed. It's a shock, a hard pill to swallow in the wake of upbringing where we are taught to be kind, ethical, and considerate to our fellow beings.

No matter how smart, how strong, or how wise you may be – if you are a good person, you may be under threat from someone who will try to exploit who you are. Some of the worst of these wolves underneath amiable sheep attire are psychopaths, sociopaths, and narcissists.

Who are These People?

The difference between a psychopath and a more everyday manipulator is that most people who do immoral things are held back by **conscience** and **personal values** so as not to exceed a certain limit. Extreme actions are usually only induced by periods of intense stress, threat, or pressure.

But with a psychopath, there are no limits; they have no internal control. People are moving objects to them. Any action – betrayal, fraud, lies, sabotage, or even murder – are possible at any time if that action may prove beneficial for them. They are loyal to no entity but themselves. They operate under a cold and calculating rationality that exploits and betrays anyone in a vulnerable situation they can take advantage of. Friends and family are just the same; it makes no difference. Without a capacity for empathy, they have no capacity to feel guilt.

It has been said that psychopaths are the most dangerous men and women on the planet. They are the saboteurs, the toxic co-workers, the deceivers, and murderers who lure you into relationships, friendships, or business partnerships specifically to use you, scam you, defraud you, decimate your reputation, or just play you for sport and entertainment.

Considering that most survivors need 12 to 24 months of recovery before they can fully trust again, you may imagine that these people are perfectly capable of inhibiting your success, career, and indeed your whole life with their sabotaging and undermining tactics.

What are the Differences between Sociopaths, Narcissists, and Psychopaths?

All of these terms refer to people who operate by means of callous manipulation. The most prominent term in the media, literature, and current research is 'psychopath'. This denotes the predatory aggressors who like to prey on and hurt others, sometimes just for fun. Clinical professionals have minute differentiations between those labels and subdivide each into additional categories.

For the purposes of simplicity in this guide, we are going to refer to all these types under the umbrella term of psychopath.

This is for three reasons:

1. There are many differing schools of thought. Clinical professional diagnostics rely on nuanced categorization, while independent practical experts and spiritual gurus treat them as the same.

2. Leaving the scientific spectrum, the common denominators for this type of dysfunction are an inability to love, no evidence of conscience or remorse, and the lack of any moral codes. At the end of the day, the label doesn't matter. It is the harmful impact of their actions on others that are of objective importance.

3. Within the scientific spectrum, the psychopath exhibits the most extreme behavior. If you know how to deal with them, you can handle the less extreme attributes of other categories, including the everyday manipulators. This book will give you an advantage over all of them.

Are There Different Types of Psychopath?

What are the differences between lower-functioning and higher-functioning psychopaths?

As with all people, there are individual differentiators between psychopaths. Here are the facts to remember:

- Psychopathy is an inborn characteristic. It's not a product of low self-esteem or poor social upbringing.

- Psychopaths exist in various social classes, in all family types, rich and poor, and may be either high-functioning or low-functioning in any context.

- A high-functioning psychopath tends to have more impulse control, enabling some self-restraint from immediately violent acts, while a low-functioning psychopath is not able to control impulse as effectively, leading to a stronger likelihood that they will exhibit extreme violent tendencies.

- The basic personality and intrinsic motivations remain unchanged, but these manifestations may be defined to some extent by socio-economic characteristics.

However:

- Psychopathic motivations are all the same.

- The ability to love is always non-existent.

- All psychopaths view other human beings as objects to be used, manipulated, and discarded.

Please note that the chart on the following page is simplified and generalized to enable a 'big picture' understanding of how psychopathic instincts, colored by education and socio-economic status, translate into behaviors. It is not absolute. Characteristics and actions can move from one position to another.

For example, a psychopath may improve their circumstances in life and move up in socio-economic standing. Yet their fundamental nature to use, manipulate, and harm will never change.

Having no conscience means that **any action** is possible for the psychopath, provided that they perceive the situation warrants it. A higher-functioning psychopath with better impulse control might not commit violence personally, but they may well hire someone else to do it.

Ability to Fit into Society	Class	Method of Operation	Education	Typical Crimes	Typically Marries For
Lower Functioning	Criminal	Extremely poor impulse control. Violent. Criminal.	High School or less.	Murder, assault, rape, burglary, drugs, gang involvement.	Sex, benefits, impulsive thrills. Abandon responsibilities.
	Parasitic	Less prone to violence. Use manipulation and deceit to get what they want. Live off others. Men generally live off of relationship with women.	High School. Possibly college drop out.	Petty crimes. Parasitic but manage to stay out of prison.	Money, shelter, sex, benefits, household services.
Higher Functioning	White Collar	Blends in at professional occupations. Can rise to high positions of power. Intrinsically loyal to self, never company. Abuse people and resources under their control.	College or higher.	Generally non-violent. White collar crimes. Investment scams, shady businesses, etc.	Community status. The exterior image of a family man. Semblance of respectability.

What are the Roots and Origins of Psychopathic Behavior?

In today's day and age, psychopathy and related disorders are classified as a psychological disorder. However, these types of people have existed throughout history.

The root of the problem is a lack of an ability to love, a deficiency which has far-reaching consequences for the psychopath's instinctual behavior and the myriad avenues of his or her life, as well as the lives of others.

Before we go further, let's define what love means, as the majority of the global population understands it. Below are definitions from various dictionaries:

Love: *noun*

1. Strong affection for another arising out of kinship or personal ties. (From the Merriam-Webster Dictionary)

2. **A deep, tender, ineffable feeling of affection and solicitude towards a person, such as that arising from kinship, recognition of attractive qualities, or a sense of underlying oneness.** (From the American Heritage Dictionary)

3. A strong feeling of affection. (From the Oxford Dictionary)

Love is a warm emotion emanating from deep within us. With the above definitions in mind, we may conclude that the ability to love and the ability to relate to one another are inseparable.

There are many side effects from this crucial inability to love:

1. When you can't love, you can't empathize with others. Instinctively, consideration of what happens to other people, their feelings, and the ability to care about the well-being of another are totally non-existent. You are capable of any action – base, seedy and outrageous – as long it makes rational sense and you can get away with it. There is zero moral compass, moral responsibility, and accountability over consequences. Remorse and guilt are alien.

2. When you can't empathize or love emotionally, you see people as nothing more than moving objects or resources to grab, utilize, or own; toys to play with; or chess pieces to maneuver. Most relationships are based upon calculated intent, to obtain a benefit or fill a need. No real emotional warmth is felt, no connection made.

3. You feel no intervening sense of obligation based on emotional attachment to others. Obligations arising from ties such as loyalty, financial commitments, family, friendship, social contracts, romantic relationships, or marriage commitments can be broken easily, completely unhindered by conscience – they were never seen as obligations to begin with.

4. There's **zero capacity** to experience rich emotional nourishment, peace, happiness, contentment, or any connection to higher sources of spiritual fulfillment. This absence of experience could cause what clinical psychologists term **perpetual boredom**, where the sufferer continually turns to new occupations and activities to escape the sense of emptiness they experience in daily life. Consequently, joy in life comes only in the form of covert and overt **domination games**, which provide a temporary thrill of 'winning'. The emotional range of a psychopath

can be described as an arousing sense of power, omnipotence, and feeling of intoxication. This is the only emotional high they are capable of experiencing, and their actions need to be perpetually repeated for the same effect. Gaining the upper hand, personal games of domination and control, sexual conquests, political takeovers, violence, bullying, and obnoxious behavior are all such ramifications.

5. The psychopath is unable to relate to people in a natural manner. Compensating mechanisms are employed by the brain for social interaction, causing two consistent behavioral ramifications:

   - Relating from the inside out, they instinctively and constantly don different masks for different audiences throughout their lives.

   - Relating from the outside in, they always deal with people as *symbols* or *representations* of others that are not even present – a generalized compartment or mold to fit into. For example, if the psychopath grew up with a 'grandma type' in their early life, and you are of the same age and appearance, the psychopath will treat you as they treated their grandma. You are expected to behave a certain way and they will treat you a certain way. If the psychopath's first boyfriend or girlfriend, or their perception of a 'boyfriend/girlfriend type', is a certain way, and you look like that type, they will treat you with that tailor-made persona, in turn applying tailor-made expectations to you.

6. In romantic relationships, the psychopath tries to maneuver people into their mold and expectations. **The ob-**

jective is to control the target's feelings, behaviors, and the outcome of the relationship. They may engage in hot and cold behavior, coming on strong and then backing off to keep the target's energy on them, engaging in psychological games of reward and punishment, and going from obsession and adoration to contempt in the blink of an eye. All this produces psychological turmoil, confusion, and emotional anguish on an unaware target.

7. No matter how successful, well-to-do, or have-it-all they seem on the surface, the psychopath may seek to hurt or destroy the things they can never possess (love and affection, and those who experience them fully) for sadistic pleasure. Since psychopaths never experience love, they may well feel no personal lack or deficiency, instead holding those who do experience affection in contempt. However, psychopaths can tell when people are happy and glowing with the power that emanates from love – a power they don't understand and can't **control** or **own**. Hence, those who emanate love, who exude **positivity**, **optimism**, and **happiness**, and those who possess **strong moral fiber** can be targets, not for what they ever did to the psychopath personally, but for who they are – the intrinsically beautiful qualities which they can't access on the earthly plane.

8. The psychopath instinctively views any social exchange as an opportunity to 'feed' upon another person. They don't seek an equal relationship, but a dominant relationship. Not being able to empathize, they are incapable of creating equality. The tools in their war chest to gain the upper hand are **hidden strategies** and **covert aggression**.

However, most people who can empathize don't go into a relationship expecting to be a supply to feed from, to be deceived, manipulated, conned, or back-stabbed. Most people go into relationships, friendships, or partnerships with trust, honesty, respect, openness, and they expect to be treated similarly in return. They have no idea they are in a covert guerrilla war.

Hence, the complete **unfairness and inequality** of the entire game. The psychopaths' (and other abusive manipulators') games for domination within relationships are **always the same**. They lure a target in by presenting a front that is the complete opposite of who they really are inside. They learn everything about the target's weaknesses for later use, while keeping their own life private. They gradually undermine the target, working behind their back while the target remains unsuspecting and trusting. Finally, the psychopath gets bored or obtains the calculated benefits, and either destroys, betrays, or discards the target. When the target finally catches on, it's usually too late. A lot of damage has been done, or the odds on getting out unharmed are overwhelmingly against them.

"Conscience never exists without the ability to love, and sociopathy is ultimately based in lovelessness."

– Martha Stout, The Sociopath Next Door

Can a Psychopath Ever Fall in Love?

If our concept of love is, in its most basic form, the ability to care about the well-being of another human being, an unselfish, loyal, and benevolent concern for the good of another, then a psychopath can **never** love in the way most of us understand it.

Most of the time a psychopath only feigns the 'job' of love to obtain calculated benefits. However, perhaps only in a few instances in a lifetime, they may consider themselves to have 'fallen in love.'

The psychopath's concept of love falls outside of both our **dictionary definitions** and **mainstream society's definitions** of love. A psychopath's concept of love is based on filling an internal hole or hunger. It is experienced as wanting something or someone very badly, intensely, and completely. It's a powerful but dark emotion with roots based in **ownership and possession**. Thus, when you are at the receiving end of a psychopath's 'love' or 'passionate obsession', they hunger for you, they want to possess you and own you as part of a collection. Such a relationship can seem quite passionate and intense in the short term, especially with society's glorification of such dynamics in some books and media. Ultimately, however, the object of 'love' will be controlled in every possible way, like a pet or possession, and be allowed **minimal or no independent will**.

There are two deep-seated mechanisms which may drive this behavior. First, an instinctive fear that they will lose their object or be abandoned. Second, a fear that their 'love' makes them powerless. Their response to the fear is to control every single aspect of the life of their object and to be the one in power. This reaction is often located on an unconscious level and may not be at the conscious level of self-awareness.

The long-term consequences of this sort of behavior is dramatic, and even tragic, as you can imagine. How do you think that pet or object will fare in the long term when continually deprived of freedom and free will? What might happen to someone who surrenders and totally capitulates to another, an individual whose primary motivation is self-benefit?

True love is unconditional and unselfish. It constitutes caring about the well-being of the other above your own – caring when it does not benefit you and may even inconvenience you. Knowing your loved one is happy brings a smile to your face, however much you are inconvenienced.

With a psychopath, this kind of true love can never be possible because their ability to relate to others is permanently impaired.

The irony is that when an obsession for a particular person does hit them, the psychopath often loses the person they 'love' by their own tactics. In a romantic relationship with a psychopath, one of the following situations is most likely to unfold:

- The partner sees the light and leaves the intolerable environment, with its unreasonable behaviors and expectations.

- The partner will be controlled and eventually tossed out when they are perceived to have undergone a loss of usefulness, physical beauty, health, or similar attributes. In such situations, the psychopath believes the partner to have become a burden which should be cast off.

- The psychopath terminates the life of the partner, just as they would destroy an object they own and no longer value.

- The partner is so controlled, drained, and possibly depressed they are driven to suicide, as the last means of voicing an independent will and escaping a reality they can no longer tolerate.

What is the Best Defense Mechanism against a Psychopath?

Embracing the reality that these people exist, spotting them, and avoiding relationships of any kind with them altogether are the absolute best preventative measures of dealing with a psychopath.

Once you are enmeshed in the hypnotic web a psychopath spins, it takes time and energy to extricate yourself. And because your needs and your feelings don't exist for the psychopath, **almost everyone gets hurt in the process**. The variables are simply how much time and effort it takes to get out, and the degree to which you are damaged.

To avoid this outcome, it's best that as soon as you spot them, you avoid them in a quiet, inoffensive manner. Remember, you are dealing with someone with a twisted mindset to whom the normal social rules and contracts can't apply. If you make any overt scenes, the psychopath, being petty and non-empathetic, will be vengeful.

In the following pages, we will examine in detail how to identify the psychopath and explore the available strategies to protect yourself and to fight against and minimize potential dangers.

How Does One Identify a Psychopath?

It's very difficult to identify a psychopath by appearance, as they are often habituated to altering personas in order to appear non-threatening. Hence, behavioral and subjective factors are usually used to identify them.

Almost all authors who have written on this topic have their own method of identifying a psychopathic or sociopathic individual. Robert D. Hare has the most widely accepted list of clinical identifiers, called the Hare Psychopathy Checklist.[2]

The goal here is to compile a structured summary for the reader, organized around realistic time constraints, social application, and overall value.

The Five-minute Method of Deciding Who to Trust

To decide who to trust in everyday situations, Martha Stout has a fast and easy rule included in her book *The Sociopath Next Door*.[3]

Look for the combination of consistently bad, outrageously inadequate, and hurtful behavior, combined with frequent 'pity plays' for your sympathy. This is a sign of a conscienceless person.

This person may not be a mass murderer per se, but it's clearly not someone you should trust with anything involving integrity and responsibility. Avoid bringing them into your intimate circle, allowing them to become your boyfriend or girlfriend, marrying them, sharing confidences, or taking them on as a business partner.

The Primary Identifying List: Five Absolute Traits All Psychopaths Have in Common

As each individual psychopath is different, in considering the characteristics of their personality, it's possible to distinguish between **relative** and **absolute** traits. Relative traits vary from person to person, but because absolute traits are observable across the board, recognizing them may help to identify someone as being a psychopath. Sheridan has the most effective **absolute** list of identifying a psychopath.[4] From his experience, Sheridan concluded that the following are the traits almost every psychopath he has researched has in common:

1. **Use of pity plays** – Invoking pity and sympathy to manipulate, control, or obtain benefits. 'Poor me' acts (such as faking serious illnesses or insisting they have been victimized in the unlikeliest of situations) produce sympathy, excuse questionable behavior, and obscure malicious motives. Healthy, non-manipulative individuals with positive intent don't often do this.

2. **No remorse** – Engaging in flagrantly amoral behavior without a second thought: betrayal, threats, or stealing; failing to show any real, consistent, or tangible signs of remorse after being discovered.

3. **Mysterious past or personal history** – This may include missing timelines, moving from state to state, even countries, under mysterious circumstances, or unexplained gaps in personal history. This may be to conceal time in prison, being on the run, involvement in drugs, multiple marriages in other states and countries, or abandoned children and spouses.

4. **High levels of the testosterone hormone** – This can manifest as a more impulsive and intense personality than other people display. An individual with high testosterone may frequently engage in fearless, attention-seeking, high-risk behavior. They may have an over-the-top sex drive or be sexually aggressive, with less concern for consent. In appearance, they may have a lot of upper body strength, and in some cases, there may be a hormone-based 'glow' about them.

5. **Invented personas** – Psychopaths have glaringly different personas for each type of person they interact with. Their brains are unable to relate to social situations intuitively. Thus, they observe others and carefully create masks to deal with certain situations or people. For instance, they create one persona for romantic interests, another for a particular group of friends, and another for work or family. Multi-faceted identities are a normal aspect of personality, but the psychopath takes this to extremes. They may fashion new personas – complete with new hair, clothes, fictional background histories, the whole works – when they are interested in a new target or scam, or when they move to a new area. All of a sudden, they are gay, an animal welfare activist, or a Wall Street type, whatever the new social scam requires.

The Hare Psychopathy Checklist

The **Hare Psychopathy Checklist** is the pre-eminent scientific diagnostic tool used to rate a person's psychopathic tendencies. It was originally developed in the 1970s by Dr Robert D. Hare for criminal offenders. Its official name is PCL-R (Psychopathy Checklist–Revised).[2]

There are two key points to note about the PCL-R:

1. It lists 20 psychopathic traits in four main domains – **Interpersonal, Emotional, Lifestyle**, and **Antisocial**.

2. The tool is points-based. This indicates that the scientific measurement of psychopathy exists on a spectrum, from minor to severe. The scoring system goes from 0 (no psychopathy) to 40 (prototypical psychopath). Most people in the general population score under 5. A cut score of 25–30 and above is typically used to identify psychopaths.

The four domains and 20 traits are summarized below:

Interpersonal – How psychopaths present themselves to others

1. Glib and superficial charm
2. Pathological lying
3. Grandiose (exaggeratedly high) estimation of self
4. Need for stimulation
5. Cunning and manipulativeness

Affective – What they feel or do not feel emotionally

6. Lack of remorse or guilt
7. Lack of empathy
8. Shallow and superficial emotional responsiveness
9. Failure to accept responsibility for own actions

Lifestyle – How they live in society

10. Parasitic lifestyle

11. Criminal versatility

12. Lack of realistic long-term goals

13. Impulsivity

14. Irresponsibility

Antisocial – Proclivity for behavior that is violent or harmful to others

15. Poor behavioral controls

16. Early behavior problems

17. Juvenile delinquency

18. Revocation of conditional release (applicable to criminals that have violated the conditions of prison release)

Other items

19. Sexual promiscuity

20. Many short-term marital relationships

The Relative Secondary Identifying List

This list encompasses valuable information collected from other sources. Much on this list may seem subjective and generalized, but if you ever meet or get to know a psychopath at a close distance, you will likely recognize more and more traits as you continue down this list.

As each psychopath is different, not all of the points on this list will apply to a given individual. Possessing one or two of these traits does not guarantee that somebody is a psychopath. The high-functioning psychopath may also possess a more developed social front.

Your instinctive feelings

1. In interacting with them, you feel chilled. You may experience a skin-crawling effect, or the hair on the back of your neck standing up.

2. In person, they just seem 'off'. It is hard for you to explain or pinpoint exactly what it is, but it won't go away.

3. If you are a naturally intuitive, empathetic individual who connects emotionally with people, you may notice that it's impossible to establish an emotional connection with them. You feel a cold emptiness rather than warmth.

4. They may seem darkly seductive, giving off a dangerous vibe.

5. Pay attention to your energy. Notice if you feel uncomfortable, tired, or exhausted. A psychopath is essentially cold in their interactions with others, and this can be socially, psychologically, and emotionally draining.

6. You feel like prey. If you are a target, they chase you in a way that violates the norms of consideration and borders the edge of propriety. They invade your personal space, come up close and focus their gaze on you, giving you little space to breathe. It can be flattering at first; you may be induced to think that they are simply fearless go-getters or confident take-chargers. But if this is making you uncomfortable, their pushiness indicates a lack of empathy and consideration for social rules.

7. When they are done with you, there may be a sense of bitterness you have never felt in more normal encounters with others, even in disagreements or parting on bad terms.

8. You can't think clearly near them. Psychopathic energy has been compared to brainwashing. The combination of body language, eyes, words, intense energy, presence, and tactics can manipulate people's emotions. Targets have reported that it takes as little as two weeks of being around a psychopath to make someone feel numb and unable to think straight, as though in a surreal world. It takes time to shake the fog off and come back to grounded safety and rationality.

Their body language

1. **Eyes: the predator stare** – If you are observant and interact frequently enough, you may notice moments of an empty, dead, piercing predator stare. The person in question may also be unusually unfazed by uninterrupted eye contact. If in sexual or romantic circumstances, the eyes are used to give off a deeply seductive vibe, which can be interpreted by targets as hypnotizing, creepy, or beautiful. It's a marked and unusual trait.

2. **They seem to talk at you, not to you** – There are three reasons for this. First, psychopaths use words to control. Second, their personas require premade scripts. Lastly, always being self-focused, psychopaths do not connect with others in the same way empaths do. They can calibrate their acting based on how people react, and they can imitate others, but that genuine spark of true empathy is missing.

3. **Eerie micro-facial expressions** – For psychopathic brains, compensating mechanisms are needed for social survival. These mechanisms may create a processing delay during social interaction, manifesting as a weird, cold, reptilian look for a couple of seconds, totally unlike the person

you thought you knew. These are flashes that happen very fast and are easy to miss.

4. **Speech and voice disfluency** – The typical psychopath's voice can be animated and excited when 'performing', but a monotone in everyday life. When asked highly detailed impromptu questions, there can be odd hesitations, such as many 'umms' and 'uhs', in the psychopath's reply. This is due to the psychopath's premade persona. When performing ready-made scripts and roles, they are prepared and unhesitatingly articulate. Otherwise, they project flat, dead, non-personalities.

Hobby and behavior

1. **Pathological lying** – Psychopaths have a weird relationship with truth. They lie about big things, small things, and things they don't need to lie about. Some seem afraid of the truth and instinctively hide it. Some actually wholeheartedly believe that whatever they say becomes truth. If you catch them in an obvious lie, this type of psychopath will just deny it and believe it never happened. The bottom line is that they want others to accept their self-serving versions of distorted reality in order to get people under their control.

2. **Charisma and charm during first meetings** – Psychopaths can come across as confident, energetic, and charismatic. As mentioned earlier, the hormone testosterone may bestow a certain 'glow' on them.

3. **Disconnects between what they say and do** – The psychopath may seem kind but engage in flagrantly inappropriate or depraved actions.

4. **Huge ego and tendency to brag** – Their sense of self-worth recalls the proverbial God Complex. The psychopath feels superior, though is frequently without substance or achievements to back it up. They tend to brag endlessly about their conquests, exploits, and 'bad' things they have done. Their need for idolization and adoration can be insatiable.

5. **Extreme promiscuity** – One-night stands, womanizing, and superficial sex are common behaviors for a psychopath. There are no sexual limits. The boundaries of the workplace, social contracts, and even statutory rape and incest are not taboo, just opportunities. Alcohol and other illegal substances may be used remorselessly to get what they want.

6. **Juggling multiple partners and new relationships immediately after a 'serious' relationship ends. Going on the prowl immediately after a breakup** – Normal people need a period of time to recover before starting afresh if the original partner had meant anything. Psychopaths do not. As no emotional ties and obligations were felt on their part, a new relationship is just new supply that can provide money, sex, entertainment, and attention. As they see people as moving objects, they are rather excited by a fresh new toy over an old one that is out of season.

7. **Parasitic** – They have no real job and live off the labors of others. This is frequently the case with lower-functioning psychopaths. A mid- or higher-functioning psychopath may take their domination games to corporate politics and business.

8. **Involvement with taking, buying, or selling drugs, or other unlawful activities** – Psychopaths typically feel at

home in drug cultures because they satisfy more than one need – their need for risk and thrills, the fast money involved, and the availability of mind-altering substances to alleviate their boredom.

9. **Unusual sleeping patterns** – Psychopaths sleep differently. First, they consistently need little sleep, at most 4–5 hours of sleep a night. Second, they fall asleep instantly and awake instantly with no fatigue, not the gradual waking process experienced by normal individuals. When they sleep, they seem 'dead', with no turning or tossing. Lastly, unlike normal people, they do not dream.

10. **No real creative talent** – They can copy but can't be original.

11. **Unsolicited favors and gestures** – This includes flattery, periods of 'love bombing' (grooming or influencing a person by lavish demonstrations of attention and affection), and gestures and gifts that seem fake. The flattery is designed to wear down defenses and ingratiate themselves with the target in order to gain trust. The love bombing is designed to boost the target up into habitual dependency in order to manipulate them in the future. Unsolicited gifts and favors are given, not to be genuine, but to buy the target, indebt them for a calculated favor at some point in the future, brand them as a possession they own, or to mold them into someone else through obligation.

Common Coincidences in Psychopathic Individuals

This third list by no means condemns some of the below-mentioned professions as a whole; rather, these are some of the areas which may appeal to a psychopathic personality. Many psychopaths study, are affiliated with, are directly involved in, or create personas in the following:

- **Psychology** – Psychopaths are fascinated with psychology. It enables them to understand how other humans think and act and gives knowledge for manipulation.

- **Espionage, special forces personnel** – These professions are perceived by the psychopath to legitimize their proclivity for dissembling, manipulating, and evaluating individuals as objects. Male psychopaths often like to present themselves as a James Bond-esque individual, often backing their image up with many unverifiable tales.

- **The navy, armed forces, military** – A lack of conscience or natural fear can be an advantage in killing and engaging in other dangerous activities, and many join the armed forces for that purpose.

- **Wall Street** – The character traits of extreme charisma, confidence, risk-taking, and a singular focus on self-interest are admired on Wall Street. Compulsive gambling also fulfills the psychopathic need for adrenalin and excitement.

- **Law and legal professions** – Psychopaths in the legal professions are unconcerned with the underlying morals of a case; their objective is winning the legal game and making a financial killing.

- **Art dealing, music industry, sports industry** – The money and competition involved in these areas is a lure for the psychopath.

Getting a Job Versus Winning a Partner – Why Does a Psychopath Treat 'Love' the Way They Do?

The psychopath's concept of getting a man or woman is very much like certain socially prevalent attitudes of getting and keeping a job, especially a job that's just a way to pay the bills. Such a candidate will engage in the following fairly normal actions in order to get hired for a job:

1. Research the company.

2. Prepare for the interview, target the résumé to the position.

3. Woo the interviewers.

4. Get hired and win the position.

5. Once they are officially 'in', the initial mass exertion of energy plummets, sometimes to the point of coasting along, just enough to eliminate the chances of being fired.

6. Use company resources and opportunity for personal ambitions.

7. Leave the existing job or company once resources and opportunity are used up, and usually move to better or higher-paying positions. Typically have an offer lined up before leaving the existing position.

Now, personal ethics aside, in this sort of situation the performance and treatment of a run-of-the-mill job is more or less an abstract concept. Most people in our society will treat people, with their emotional ties and obligations, differently than an abstract concept.

But remember how a psychopath views people as nothing but moving objects? A human being/relationship and a position/object are intrinsically the same to them – a situation to conquer, use, and leave. Thus, to get a man or woman, a psychopath will follow the same steps.

The Relationship-as-Job Analogy

Step 1: Research the company.

The psychopath will: Research the target, assess what the target can provide – money, sex, shelter, and so on. They will master listening, and elicit information about the target's values, hopes and dreams. If the goal is marriage, they research or elicit information on the target's finances and the likely payoff for them in investing their time. They aim to understand everything that makes the target tick to create a mental image of the target's ideal partner and needs.

Step 2: Prepare for the interview, target the résumé to the position.

The psychopath will: Create a dream persona based upon gathered information. They base everything on the target's requirements.

Step 3: Woo the interviewers.

The psychopath will: Woo the target. In the 'interview' stage, they will present as a perfect candidate. Charm, attention, gifts, and love bombing will all be employed. The psychopath tends to move things fast, as they won't be able to keep up the initial act for long.

Step 4: Get hired and win the position.

The psychopath will: Win the target. The relationship is made official through marriage or moving in.

Step 5: Once they are officially 'in', the initial mass exertion of energy plummets, sometimes to the level of coasting along to avoid being fired.

The psychopath will: Immediately change their persona and behavior. At this point, they will do as little as possible, just enough to string the target along and avoid 'supply cutoff' (the target leaving). There will be an increase in controlling and manipulative behavior, designed to stabilize, control, and exploit the supply, and a decrease in affection or loving behavior. Apparent affection or niceness will be used to reward behavior they approve or to temporarily gain sympathy.

Step 6: Use company resources and opportunity for personal ambitions.

The psychopath will: Exploit the target's resources (money, property, sex, connections, etc.) until they are drained.

Step 7: Leave the existing job or company once resources and opportunity are used up.

The psychopath will: Leave or discard the target once resources are used up. They will typically have a new target lined up before leaving the existing one.

Now, an individual's behavior, performance, and utilization of a job will differ. Similarly, a psychopath's individual treatment of the 'romance situation' will differ, but more or less follow the same pattern.

The relationship-as-job analogy provides the insight necessary to understand the logic of a psychopath's approach to romance. Now we can see why such behavior exists, how a persona designed to work a target or situation is like a carefully crafted piece of theatre, and all for a specific purpose (targeting the résumé to the position). We can see why exactly the same pattern is followed for the next target. And we can see why the psychopath will remorselessly blame the target if the relationship fails. They feel they can say, *"You're the one who hired me for the job."*

To get out of such a relationship, think about the strategies companies employ to get 'problem employees' to leave without creating harmful, reverberating drama. It may be possible to engineer a situation where the psychopath leaves the situation willingly. We will cover a few ways to do this in the following chapters.

Why do Psychopaths Want to Control You Through 'Love'?

Love is the deepest and most powerful bond humans can form with each other.

When you are in love, you are capable of:

- Self-sacrifice – acting against your own best interest. Investing tremendous personal energy and time to help someone without receiving in kind.

- Giving or sharing your house, your worldly goods, your money, without bartering or exchanging for something of equally tangible value in return (which you would do in a rational, business situation).

- Staying in a confining relationship, even when it causes you pain, hurt, stress, and discomfort.

- Jumping right back into 'trying again', despite seeing and suffering obvious red flags, such as hurt, pain, and losses.

- Acting irrationally – doing things that make no logical sense.

People's actions and choices are naturally emotion-driven. What other human bond can inspire someone to do all these things out of their own free will?

Psychopaths don't understand what love actually is, but they want to exploit the associated benefits. Instead of working to acquire things honestly, they see the manipulation of intimate relationships as an easy shortcut to gain their ends. To a psychopath, the following are just tools for controlling someone to do their bidding:

- Bonds of attachment

- People's sentiments

- The individual's reactive emotional buttons

In short, what psychopaths are after is power over someone – gained by manipulating the feelings of love.

The lesson to be learned is that your affections and emotional capital are valuable resources. Be strong, be discerning. Do not give this gift to anyone who does not deserve it.

What are the Dangers and the Long-term Outcomes of Associating Closely with Psychopaths, Sociopaths, and Narcissists?

When you associate in the long term with disordered individuals, the outcome is **almost always** negative, disillusioning, or even tragic. There are very few exceptions. This is due to three reasons:

1. A psychopath's aptitude for moral depravity is a bad influence for anyone wishing to live a peaceful and conscientious life. The old proverb rings true: you become like those you associate with – for the good and the bad.

2. Psychopaths like to exploit and cheat the people closest to them. The frequent pattern of those closest to them getting hurt or being driven to ruin is often observable by outsiders.

3. They can even harm and hurt you *unintentionally*, because none of their actions or decisions take others' welfare into account. For example:

   - The majority of HIV patients who regularly have **sex without protection** are psychopaths. They simply don't care about anything other than obtaining sex for themselves.

   - Psychopathic husbands regularly cheat outside of marriage, contract diseases, and bring them back to their wives without any sense of responsibility or remorse.

   - Many spouses of psychopaths are driven to psychological problems.

- If you work with or for a psychopath, they may use you as an enabler or accomplice in their illegal scams or domination games by lying to you or withholding critical information. They are naturally reckless and don't think things through, so the danger of being caught is quite high. No thought will be paid to the potential consequences of their actions, which may endanger or negatively impact your life.

What is the Worst That Can Happen?

This question needs to be taken very seriously. Two concepts are at work here:

1. Every human being on earth feels momentary anger, rage, annoyance, and other negative feelings for those closest to them at various times. However, what prevents most people from destroying those whom they love is the emotional bond of attachment. Psychopaths lack the ability to form this bond altogether.

2. It's a documented fact that most victims of psychopaths are those that are closest to them. Family, friends, spouses, those in relationships with them, and associates are the people most in danger.

You are essentially an **object** to a psychopath. Considering their cold, rational, calculating decision processes, if there was ever a situation where the payoff of your demise is higher than having you around, and they can get away with it, what do you think they might choose to do? It's an easy decision for such disordered individuals. Without the emotional bond of attachment, or the appropriate psychological support in place, along with low-impulse control, anything can happen at any time.

Here are some examples:

1. In 2012, a well-to-do middle-class Colorado man was arrested for pushing his wife off a cliff during a hike and making it look like an accident. They had been married for 12 years. The payoff was three life insurance policies, purchased behind his wife's back, totaling $4.5m. The evidence pointed to premeditation, with a previous accident, death, and insurance collection of another wife 17

years prior. He apparently had researched his fiancée's financial status before marrying her and feigned having a job and a wealthy lifestyle. All the signs of the psychopath were there – extremely controlling behavior, obsession with money, high testosterone levels, arrogant sense of superiority, and questionable job history and sources of income.

2. In 1971, John List was fired from his job and the bills mounted up. He covered up the situation from his wife, mother, and three children. For months, he feigned having a job and went to 'work' every morning. Somewhere along the line, he decided the best option was to kill his entire family and start over with a new identity. One day he came home from his pretend job and calmly and methodically shot his entire family before leaving to make a new life for himself on the other side of the country. He likely viewed his family as objects he owned and calculated the cost of killing everyone as less than options such as divorce and child support responsibilities. List was captured in 1989. His new family had no idea of his past.

3. In 1998, during a romantic vacation in Egypt, English chemist John Allan slipped cyanide into his girlfriend Cheryl Lewis's gin and tonic drink. The poison led to an immediate and gruesome death. Allan had been parasitically living off of his wealthy girlfriend for 4–5 years and had no other source of income. Cheryl's will, worth £490,000, was forged, leaving Allan the sole beneficiary. Police dug through a convoluted array of fabricated lies, tales, and spy fantasies before finding the truth and arresting him in 1999. Within weeks of the death of Cheryl, Allan had begun dating another wealthy woman, a di-

vorcee and Cheryl's friend. The new girlfriend began suffering from mysterious stomach ailments and was also planning to vacation with him in Egypt just prior to his arrest.

There are many more small-timers in history – people who demonstrate less overtly horrific, yet still chilling instances of self-consumed, affectionless behavior.

One thing we can glean from these examples is to be cautious before giving your heart and full trust to someone of questionable character. For instance, if there is ever a mention of life insurance money coinciding with a questionable character and suspicious activity, that is a giant red flag warning you to take extreme precautions for your safety.

Can a Psychopath Change? Will Counseling Help?

Most experts from all schools of thought agree on one thing – in 99% of cases, a psychopath cannot change.[5] Reformation really is a lost cause.

Traditional counseling, or *any type* of externally-driven influence, will not help because psychopaths lack two key personality ingredients:

1. Motivation to tell truth

2. Genuine desire to change

Mainstream counselors rely on the honest disclosure of personal information in order to prescribe effective therapy. However, the inherent nature of psychopaths means that they are wired to lie and con in all contexts of relating; they are always looking for that angle to dominate, control, and manipulate. For them, relating to the counselor is no different than relating to all human beings.

What normally happens in this situation is that the therapist receives from the psychopath half-truths or outright lies, giving an incomplete or erroneous picture to work with. Prescribed treatment is then effectively garbage in, garbage out.

Any treatment that relies on the patient being truthful runs counter to the psychopath's instinctual method of operation.

The psychopath also lacks any genuine desire to change. They do not believe there is anything wrong with them. Therapy is typically just for show, or for other covert, self-serving motives. Without an inner, driven desire, there is no sincere effort.

Chapter 2
Methods of Operation

"For the great majority of mankind are satisfied with appearance, as though they were realities and are often more influenced by the things that seem than by those that are."

– Niccolò Machiavelli

Psychopaths are most often encountered either at work or in romance. Therefore, this chapter focuses on those two social situations. We will systematically disassemble the psychopath's method of operation in each sphere.

What are the Psychopath's General Methods of Operation?

Psychopaths are actually very predictable. Wherever you encounter them, their motives are simple and unvarying. They may be hidden, like dead wood under thick layers of glossy paint, beneath a flashy image, sob stories, kind words that make them seem like a person of integrity. But no matter how deeply hidden, the true nature does exist and will emerge in time.

Rules to remember:

1. A psychopath is incapable of exertion for others' welfare. Everything they do, under any pretense, are investments made to satiate their immediate needs and desires.[1,2]

2. In any social situation, whether you meet them at work, in romance, family relationships, or landlord and tenant

situations, for the psychopath it is always a game of control and domination.

3. **A psychopath gets you within their power through deception.** Predators are incapable of openly communicating what they want via an equal relationship of give and take. They are wired to manipulate and con. They can go to great lengths to propagate a surface story which explains their motivation, but it will not be what they are really after underneath.

4. **Any assistance you give to a psychopath will only be repaid by treachery.** From their viewpoint, you are nothing but supply to be used up. The differences in each situation are **target awareness** and progression of **time.**

5. Many will habitually use the following phrases as part of their outward personality. But it's just a mantra, only word deep; it never signifies what is actually practiced.

"...In the best interests of the children and their future."

"...For the sake of our relationship and our future."
"...For the good of the family and our future."
"...In the best interests of the team/company/city/country and its future."

The Stages of Psychopathic Relationships

Wherever you encounter them, psychopathic relationships consistently advance in the following three stages:

1. Idealize/Assessment Stage

2. Devalue/Manipulation Stage

3. Discard/Abandonment Stage

The relationship can occur in a matter of months or years; it can be work-related or based on a friendship, an affair, a long-term relationship, or marriage. However, the basic nature of the psychopath's capacity for social function never changes.

They want you to be:

- Unbalanced
- Unhinged
- Weak, confused, feeling inferior
- In love with them and under their power (particularly for a romantic relationship)

So that they can:

- Dominate
- Control
- Gain a source of supply for their own ends
- Achieve a temporary thrill, euphoria, and sense of superiority for 'winning'
- Achieve complete capitulation of another person so that they can feel powerful and secure
- Entertain themselves by watching you suffer

What motivates them?

- Money
- Power
- Control
- Sex
- Winning
- Getting something for nothing
- Materialistic possessions and practical things (like a place to live)

- Ego supply and admiration

What is the psychopath afraid of?

Psychopaths are prey to the following fears:

- Fear of exposure
- Fear of losing control
- Fear of loss of supply

From the list above, we may also add the following as deep fears:

- Rejection
- Abandonment

It has been reported that many psychopaths feel rejection and abandonment keenly, as if they are in physical pain.

Although rejection and abandonment may hurt psychopathic individuals, never play with this fear intentionally or carelessly, or to settle the score. Always remember that you are **not** dealing with a normal individual with normal sensibilities and normal reactions. You are dealing with someone who is essentially mentally ill, someone without internal controls. The consequences can be dangerous. Faced with narcissistic injury, psychopaths tend to respond with extreme rage and vindictiveness. Targets that are unaware or vulnerable have been killed solely so the perpetrator can re-establish feelings of omnipotence and control.

Do they know they are psychopaths?

Most do not. They simply don't have the self-awareness and act out of sheer primal instinct. If you are born without empathy and have no understanding of how to relate affectionately to another person, how would you possibly have a taste of what you are missing?

A small minority do seem to know. However, they don't see that there is anything wrong with them and believe their traits make them superior to the rest of the human race.

What social skills do psychopaths use to get what they want?

Psychopaths are extremely predictable. They have a limited social and interpersonal repertoire. They use three general interpersonal skills and usually follow them in the same stages:

1. Charm and bribery
2. Manipulation and deception
3. Fear and intimidation

What emotions do they manipulate?

Psychopaths manipulate two primary emotions, as most people are ruled by them in their waking life. These are:

- Love
- Fear

The psychopath does not feel those emotions. They aim to control others by bombarding with fake 'love' and attention or installing 'fear'.

Method of Operation in the Workplace

Forget about what you think you know about getting ahead at work.

Simplistic career advice tells people to focus on being competent, doing a good job, and getting along with colleagues and bosses. A broader, equally important dimension is to watch out and protect yourself from backhanded attacks, such as emotional or psychological abuse and rivals spreading disinformation and outright lies. These threats are very real, but frequently unseen.

In their groundbreaking book, *Snakes in Suits: When Psychopaths Go to Work,* Babiak and Hare carefully detailed the workplace psychopath's strategy to manipulate co-workers and climb their way to the top.[3]

Psychopaths exist in many professional milieus. In a work setting, the parasitic psychopath enters a new arena. Now, instead of operating in the wider socio-economic levels of society, they need to operate within the confines and rules of a modern organization.

Corporations and other types of professional organizations each have their own culture, official and unofficial rules, and team subcultures.

However, the psychopathic nature does not change. This is simply a new platform to operate in. Once the psychopath figures out the internal mechanics of an organization, their manipulation game begins.

How they get in:

1. Psychopaths go where the action is. This means getting access to positions, organizations, and situations with

money, power, status, and excitement to be gained, and the potential for interpersonal relationships to exploit. Loving chaos and the adrenalin rush, many gravitate to fast-paced industries.

2. While many people exaggerate on their job applications, psychopaths are completely brazen deceivers. They can make up entire résumé histories, references, skills, even diplomas and certificates, to qualify for positions for which they are not qualified.

3. They make strong impressions in person. Since most hiring practices are based on interview performances in a single day, a person's true competence and character are simply assumed based on a false first impression. Psychopaths can come across as dashing, confident, capable candidates, with the potential for inspirational leadership.

What they want:

The psychopath's primary objective is to increase power, money, control, prestige, and fame for ego-aggrandizement, as well as opportunities for game-playing and thrills.

In the modern organization, with its inherent explicit structure and implicit rules, the psychopath's secondary objective is to look for *tools* and other *objects of utility* to obtain their main aims. These *objects of utility* are people that can provide:

- Informal power (people that hold influence, respect, and sway among peers without an official position)[4]

- Access to information (such as intimate knowledge of high-level executive decisions – sources may be information from executive assistants, the office grape-vine, and personnel details)

- Access to communication networks
- Influence and authority
- Power and protection
- Specialized technical knowledge if necessary to their aims (such as coding, engineering, data systems, or legal know-how)

They will not be concerned with or motivated by:

- The true benefit of the company
- Satisfaction of a job well done
- The personal welfare of other employees
- The career of other employees

Their Practical Methods of Operation

Psychopaths gain organizational power in a systematic and instinctive manner. They spend extensive time and energy behind the scenes toward building a strong influence network.

As originally noted by Babiak and Hare, as social predators, the psychopath's deceptive strategy pervades all aspects of their lives in the same cycle of **assessment, manipulation,** and **discard.**[5]

Here is their MO in an organizational setting:

Assessment

1. They use the early months of employment to study the socio-political structure of the company and try to meet as many people as they can to collect information. This includes identifying key players and personalities, the communication network, and the culture.

2. During this stage, they instinctively assess people's value and utility, then divide them into three categories – potential **patrons**, **pawns**, and the **useless**.[6] Patrons are key decision makers with high-level positions, influence, and power. They will not typically have a direct line of command and contact with the psychopath, but they can offer future protection and support. Pawns are those at closer hierarchical levels that can provide specific resources, such as information, funding, contacts, expertise, staffing, influence, and so on. Those that have little utility in the eyes of the psychopath are generally ignored.

Manipulation

3. For patrons, the psychopath ignores the normal chain of command. They brazenly capitalize on any opportunity, whether it's in the hallway or elevator, at the golf club, and other occasions offered by being a new hire, to make contact. The goal is to establish a positive presence and the image of an ambitious ideal employee and future leader. Being a master of impression management, the psychopath orchestrates each single contact with power-holders so well that some patrons eventually begin to advocate for them. Certain high-level position-holders may eventually take the psychopath under their wing to help them progress through the organization. Once this

relationship is established, over time those power-holders provide strong voices in support of the psychopath's advancement and protect them from naysayers.

4. For the pawns identified as resource providers, the psychopath gives overtures of friendship with charm and charisma to convince them of the psychopath's pleasant persona. The ultimate goal is to establish networks of personal (typically intimate) relationships to use for favors later on.

   Quite often, the psychopath will target and build strong relationships with people with *informal power* – those with a lot of influence and respect in the organization, but not necessarily the titles. The goal isn't genuine friendship but achieving maximum utility and exploitation.

   First, the psychopath gains credibility by association. Second, under the impression of an intimate friendship, those informal leaders assist the psychopath in many ways, using their influence and credibility to support them.

5. Once the players are identified, the machinations begin. The game is to manipulate people to their own ends – usually to gain more power, advancement, money, even excitement. The psychopath will manipulate communication networks to boost their own reputation, defame others, and stir conflict and rivalries among departments. They will also derail and sabotage the careers of rivals and co-workers behind their backs. As noted by Babiak and Hare, the psychopath uses two main tools:

- *Secrecy* for behind-the-scenes, subcriminal activities.

- *Shrewd impression management* to convince people of their outward persona, typically one characterized by honesty, sincerity, character – an ideal employee and even a future leader.[7]

Discard

6. When the playing fields shift, people's utility to the psychopath can change. When a previous pawn loses their utility, the psychopath will go completely cold. For normal people, estrangement in relationships tends to be gradual, with some retention of warmth and cordiality. The psychopath's discard is dramatic and chilling. All of a sudden, their previous persona shifts to one of total coldness and disdain. Targets report feeling worthless or profoundly empty, as if they are nothing. The social predator is naturally wired to create this effect, and they are consistent in all their behaviors. Unfortunately, this target reaction is probably one of the best ways to identify a psychopath at work. The effects on targets are usually shock, self-blame, and psychological turmoil, along with a sense of having lost what turned out to be a fictional friendship. Meanwhile, the psychopath moves their attention to new sources of supply.

7. In some cases, prior to discarding, the psychopath engages in character assassination behind the target's back. The goal is to pre-emptively neutralize the former target in case they seek any retribution for being used. Discrediting the target first ensures that anything they say won't be believed.

The Consequence of Colluding with Psychopaths

As social predators, psychopaths exploit all intimate relationships. In the work sphere, there are a number of consequences of intimate association to note:

1. If you are a high-potential, high-caliber employee under the authority of a psychopath, the latter will present ostensible aims of developing you for your future success. Perhaps, for example, by giving you challenging work. On the surface, it seems like great management practice; however, recall that psychopaths aim to possess, own, and drain any valuable objects for their own use. They have no sincere interest in your growth or long-term success. To secure their *possessions*, psychopaths use **isolation** and **deception**. A scenario will evolve in which they simultaneously use your work to enhance their reputation and present you with a facade of future successes, while behind your back they will sabotage and stunt your success and career options. The goal is to be the only person who can own you. Targets often don't discover this until it's too late.

2. If you collude closely with a psychopath, such as by bending rules or covering for them as 'friends', you do so at your own risk. They will almost inevitably use the information against you, selling you out when they decide your utility has expired. Normal people return favors due to an intervening sense of obligation and loyalty but giving conscienceless predators this leverage places *you* in danger.

3. Being a patron of a psychopath, your utility may be longer-range. Therefore, it will take a while to uncover disloyalty and deception. However, no matter how much a

patron advocates or protects the psychopath, once the socio-political environment shifts and a psychopath decides a protector is no longer useful to them, they have no qualms in using intimate knowledge to stab someone in the back for personal benefit. Unaware power-holders may find their position to be usurped or otherwise harmed by the psychopath they once protected and trusted.

Psychopathic Weapons of Attack and Warfare Tactics

Psychopaths use several tactics when attacking their targets. In the following section, we summarize and analyze those behaviors, so we can combat them effectively.

Psychopaths attack their targets by the following MO:

1. **To directly harm and attack you:** Psychopaths create an intolerable environment and use underhanded behaviors to cause emotional and psychological harm.[8]

a) **Emotional abuse** – Leads to feelings of anxiety, stress, depression, fear, and the inability to sleep or think straight.

A simple example is a boss engaging in direct verbal assault, yelling and swearing to tear down people's self-esteem and creating a fearful, anxious climate. A more insidious example is someone making snide jokes in public so that everyone laughs or reacts – but at your expense. Their attacks appear innocent in intention, all in good fun, and confuse you with hot and cold behavior. Their words are calculated to make you feel unhinged and wanting to explode, while keeping you restrained and silent for fear of being painted as over-sensitive or over-reacting.

b) **Psychological abuse** – Leads to feelings of low self-esteem, insecurity, lowered confidence, self-doubt, confusion, and psychological pain.

A common example is someone offering superficial public statements of outward support but engaging in relentless undermining at the same time. They achieve this by withholding key information, manipulating stakeholders to hasten deadlines, and sabotaging key resources, including setting up conflicts of people against the target. Situationally, their manipulations and acts of omission will result in missed deadlines, significant numerical miscalculations, and the loss of clients and contracts. Psychologically, this results in heightened stress, confusing feelings of chaos and imbalance, and loss of control.

There are many tactics to beget these feelings and outcomes. Even when the relationship seems cordial on the surface, or when the tactics are extremely subtle, the abuses are not accidental or due to temporary misunderstandings. They are purposeful, deliberate, and malicious. The objective is to gain control, exert power, or achieve elimination. The psychopath wants to weaken, devastate, and minimize the target so that they are mentally and emotionally off-balance, disoriented, and unable to function at full caliber.

2. **To indirectly derail people's careers or neutralize perceived rivals:** The psychopath will attack two aspects of your reputation: your **competence** and your **loyalty**.[9] Typically, this will be achieved by spreading disinformation and planting seeds of doubt amongst their own influence network. This negative press is done behind your back, so the chances of career advancement and other opportunities are thus impaired without your being aware that others might have doubts and concerns. In describing you, terms like 'ineffective manager' or 'problem employee' are common.

   a) **Attacking your competence** – They will engineer situations that make you seem incompetent and unfit for your position or spread rumors and lies to attack your effectiveness and style.

   b) **Attacking your loyalty and character** – They will do their best to cast suspicions or doubt on your loyalty, intentions, character, and dedication to the organization and its goals.

3. **The most common tactics used are:**

   a) **Planting and spreading disinformation** – Starting rumors and scandals and creating negative press without your knowledge. They do this to knock rivals out of contention. Another common tactic is to derail communication and trust and start conflicts between targeted parties and departments.

b) **Sabotage** – This includes setting someone up to fail, planting false evidence, or assigning blame to you, while frequently being complimentary, flattering, and very helpful on the surface.

c) **Covert and overt intimidation** – Psychopaths easily resort to bullying, intimidating behavior, and making veiled threats and gag orders (if they are in a position of authority), especially when charm does not work.

d) **Bribery and blackmail** – Psychopaths operate in secrecy, which enables the use of tools like bribery and blackmail behind the scenes. Sex and sexual affairs are a common psychopathic weapon used to control, bribe, and influence powerful stakeholders. Psychopaths also make grand promises to string people along, but very little will actually materialize.

What You Can Do About It

Choosing how to deal with a psychopath depends on the situation, the specific culture of the organization, and your own personality type. There is no one-size-fits-all solution. However, below are your best weapons, plus some tips to succeed and survive at work.

Assessment Prevention

Succeeding at work requires more than just technical competency. It also means taking the time to accurately access the socio-political structure of the organization you are operating in.

1. Contrary to popular belief, when you first arrive in the unfamiliar environment of a new job, avoid drawing too much attention to yourself. As originally advised by Al Mualla in How to Manipulate the Manipulator, one should use caution during the initial stages of an unfamiliar environment or encounter.[10] People are not always who they appear to be, and you could have unknown enemies and future opponents. Part of your tactics is to make them underestimate you.

This approach goes against both our natural inclination to make a great first impression and our enthusiasm to stand out. However, if you set out to be totally impressive from day one, you may generate resentment and jealousy in your colleagues and be seen as a potential threat. This impairs your future progress and success. You will also make it hard to work unnoticed and unchallenged. Therefore, it's most prudent to stay under people's radar initially. Instead use this critical time for observation – to correctly assess the political environment and determine the most effective method of operation. After that, may come the time to shine.

Before your utility and identity are out in the open, make careful assessments of how those around you treat others. Take note of who treats everyone the same, as a reflection of their genuine personality. Many others may treat people differently on a continuum – due to shyness, busyness, status, snobbishness, or other reasons. They are not necessarily psychopathic. Psychopaths are drastically different. When you have no perceived value or utility, their aloofness can be chilling. By contrast, they will instantly exhibit a persona of charm only when they perceive you to hold value.

The important thing is never to operate blindly when heading into a new environment.

2. Learn to recognize that there are characters very different from your own – the wolves in sheep's clothing. Those who are seemingly unthreatening (perhaps even ingratiating) in early meetings, but have an unusual career trajectory, extreme polarity in people's assessments of and reaction to them, extreme hot and cold demeanors to different people, or have kept a specific position or influence within the company for an unusually long time, need to be carefully observed. There is probably a good reason for their power. They could be genuinely steadfast loyalists to the company or they might be territorial, dirty fighters who have maintained control and position by more cunning means than others. Covert predators succeed because they stay close to the ground and are careful to appear calm, collected, quiet, and unthreatening

before they strike. The intended victims never see what's coming until it's too late.

3. Psychopaths covet power and control, regardless of the expense to others. In organizational settings, this can manifest as the use of incoherent, inefficient, and confusing systems, both to keep others off balance and to make themselves indispensable by manufactured dependency. As a well-intentioned empath, before you try to instill positive changes, it's wise to test and assess people's receptiveness to small changes first. Then carefully probe their deeper motivations. Sincere intentions for improvements are an asset, but you need to make sure the socio-political environment supports it. Otherwise, you can be completely blindsided by covert territorial warfare and control games.

Even non-psychopaths may take time to warm up to changes. The difference is that psychopaths are impervious to rational discussion if the perceived improvements threaten their control.

Relationship Prevention

The emphasis on competition, survival, and organizational politics within modern organizations encourages behaviors motivated by self-interest. They can be breeding grounds for people who will do anything, without empathy or remorse.

In the confines of the workplace, information is power, and workplace relationships are how information travels. Hence, you need to be fully conscious of where information is going – both the outflow and the intake.

Unless a relationship at work has been proven over a long period of time, it helps to be a little distrustful of everyone in the work arena. Here are three points of how relationships, information, and machinations are intimately tied:

1. Many people look to find 'friends' at work. In many environments, over the long term, this can be a mistake. Opening up too quickly makes a person vulnerable to manipulators directly, or vulnerable for private information to be shared with people who will abuse it. At the workplace, one should differentiate and establish clear boundaries between workplace allies (those you are friendly to for mutual support and a positive reputation) and intimate friends (those you tell your secrets to). In most cases, it's best to find your friends elsewhere and just go to work for professional advancement and the paycheck.

2. Keep your weaknesses to yourself or to those you trust outside of the work circle. When you are in a desperate situation, never tell psychopathic personalities anything personally significant, such as members of your family being ill. They will exploit anyone in a one-down position, take gross advantage of them, and may use any vulnerability to destroy or manipulate their competitors.

3. Modern organizations constitute a framework in which your managers can change frequently. While building a relationship with your boss is key, it also helps to avoid taking everything they say blindly at face value. For example, all too commonly people use language that suggests that everything they do is for the good of the company, but their underlying motives are power and control. Independently assess each of your new boss's personality, career trajectory, motives, and goals, then independently verify any important information you are being told. Understanding the real agenda and underlying

motives has two benefits: it prevents you from falling into hidden traps where you can be blamed; and you can gain your superior's support by 'selling' to their interest.

Behavioral Tactics and Prevention

1. Your self-control is your best weapon. If you suspect someone is a psychopath, carefully observe their tactics and methods of operation for effective countermeasures. Do not overtly oppose or confront them. Direct opposition sets you up as a target to neutralize. Avoid this, for example, by telling them what they want to hear overtly, while acting to your own advantage covertly.

2. The best strategy for dealing with psychopaths is to avoid them altogether. The second best is to keep your distance and minimize contact. But what if you can't avoid them and have to work with them? The third best strategy is to ensure the positives you bring to the organization are always proportionally greater in the value and utility scale than potential negatives – either real or caused by your detractors and rivals.

The reality is that most modern organizations, and especially for-profit corporations, hire and retain people based on utility and value to the organization. No matter what the PR says – customer service, integrity, value – the core value is usually money, and how everyone directly or indirectly contributes to the bottom line.

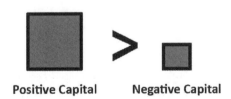

Positive Capital   **Negative Capital**

Positive capital in the above diagram denotes your competence, reputation, workplace allies, and influence, value-added initiatives that help key organizational goals, strong and trustworthy relationships with your superiors, and specialized, hard-to-replace, industry know-how. Negative capital is anything that detracts from your value to the organization, such as immaturity, lack of punctuality, unreliable behaviors, tempers that create enemies, any kind of poor reputation among peers, strained relationships with key functions, poor or non-existent relationship with leadership, and so on.

You need to actively manage your value scale. First, you need to control and minimize all your behaviors that contribute to the negative capital block.

Contact with psychopaths or those with tendencies approaching psychopathic behavior *indirectly* falls under the negative. Their proclivity for blaming, sabotaging, and stealing credit means increased risk of negative perception. If you come under the influence of a psychopath, you can get a transfer, minimize your role, distance yourself, or employ other shrewd tactics to reduce risk. If you don't work with them and avoid assignments under their control, blame and sabotage are minimized. Avoid certain traps – not all assignments and positions are equally desirable.

To increase your positive capital, you can widen your circle of influence, gain allies, and focus your energy on projects where *you can control the outcome*. This also means being vigilant about your reputation. Upon hearing certain negative perceptions about yourself, counteract them immediately and strategically – go into active campaign mode in the communication networks to promote positive perceptions.

3. Be patient. Psychopaths are naturally impulsive, reckless, and need bigger and bigger domination games to feel a thrill. Eventually, they venture that one step too far and get caught. Being cautious and patient enables you to keep a level head and decide what your best course of action is without rushing.

4. Depending on how toxic the situation is, sometimes the best solution is to leave the job and the company. It can be a waste of time, energy, and emotional capital to fight psychopathic machinations, rather than achieving constructive results in positive environments. The reality is that psychopathic personalities are a completely different breed, immune to logical discussion and poison to be close to. In those situations when you no longer have anything to lose, maximize the impact of your confidential exit interviews to people who matter and can be trusted. This may be the only opportunity to bring hidden machinations to light.

Investigative Tactics

1. Psychopaths frequently lie and fake credentials on their résumés. A secret background check may tell you what you need to know. Take care to act anonymously if you wish to expose them. They are extremely vindictive.

2. In some situations, the methods of the criminal detective may apply to gather evidence. If you wish to use recording devices and tools, be sure to check your local and state laws to understand and avoid illegality.

3. Corporate veterans advise that a reputation-ruining scandal may be the best and only way to oust an entrenched psychopath. While many psychopaths do eventually depart as a by-product of scandal, this is a controversial topic. There are two factors to consider. First, assess your own level of wherewithal to pull it off. Second, psychopaths have a need to win at all costs and one should never underestimate how far, and how low they are willing to go. If the identity of the perceived threat is known, they will retaliate with shocking vengeance. It may very likely be your own good name that will be ruined. Make sure that whatever you do is anonymous, that it can't be traced back to you, and that the evidence is irrefutable.

Method of Operation in Romantic Relationships

"No person is your friend who demands your silence or denies your right to grow."

– Alice Walker

Among all the situations in which you can encounter a psychopath, arguably the most emotionally destructive and dangerous is a close personal relationship. Here, in this realm, is where they truly become psychotic.

Why This is Dangerous

We go into love relationships with our hearts open, honestly exposing our vulnerabilities for a genuine emotional connection. It's unusual to go into a love relationship expecting another person to hurt and destroy you purposefully for sadistic pleasure, or to drain you dry for credit, money, sex, shelter, or property, before discarding you.

This is why the playing field is completely unequal from the beginning. For the empath, the relationship will be about love, openness, happiness, and companionship. For the psychopath, the relationship is about utility, control, power over the other, and ownership. When one side openly shares, the other is constantly performing interpersonal calculus – mentally calculating how to use that information in the future to manipulate, intimidate, sabotage, or threaten, so as to hold on to any self-motivated benefits they originally calculated when they started the relationship.

Emotional and psychological pain can last far longer than physical pain. Most people never fathom how deeply they can be damaged psychologically and emotionally; they have a blind spot leaving them wide open for this type of predator. A psychopathic predator usually tries to inflict the maximum emotional damage possible.

What they want:

The psychopath will be motivated by:

- Money, credit cards, and credit score to obtain material goods

- Sex

- Shelter or the lifestyle you can provide

- The semblance and image of respectability and normalcy

- Power – the psychopath wants power over people, and they confuse that with love. Seducing and conquering gives them a euphoric thrill of winning

- Control – controlling, bending, and harming others give them meaning in life

- Ego-aggrandizement and admiration

They won't be motivated or bothered by:

- Love

- What is best for you or your welfare

- Your happiness

- A desire to help you or see you succeed

Their Actual Method of Operation

The romance game for the psychopath can be summarized as the following: a protracted scam; a toxic combination of fake love and real abuse.

The psychopath presents themselves first as the opposite of who they really are, while assessing the benefits of the target. Once they've got the target on the hook, the psychological warfare begins, with the end goal to use, control, and dominate. But the target won't suspect these motives in what seems a blissful romantic relationship; initially, their investment and feelings are real. The emotional investments will remain real as the target struggles to hold on to the romantic fantasy that is slowly turned into a nightmare. Once the psychopath has drained all the value they can from the target – once the target is no longer useful – they are discarded *cold*. There will be no closure given, no remorse, no affection, no caring or compassion for the target's well-being, even if the relationship lasted decades.

For the target, the beginning may be beautiful and euphoric, but the ending will be bitter and excruciatingly soul-destroying.

Expect the following at the assessment/idealize stage: The perfect appearance of a genuine person

- A guise of a kind-hearted, perfect man or woman.

- Displays of moral outrage on social issues, whatever they pick up on as important to you – truth, justice, the standard of behavior of other people, how men treat women, and so on – so as to come across as completely decent and admirable.

- Tales of victimization from a previous relationship, with their ex painted as crazy, mean, psychotic, and so on. Sometimes flattering comparisons between you and their ex. *This is a pity play to elicit sympathy and also a manipulative tactic to subtly influence your behavior and motivate you to surpass their ex.*

The contrast of assessment and 'love bombing'

- Lots of probing questions for a careful assessment of your value. They are looking for what you have for them, how easy it would be to take it from you, what unfulfilled needs you have that they can use to lure you into a commitment, and what weaknesses you have that they can target and manipulate.

- Over-the-top love bombing, including incessant attention, flattery, gifts, whirlwind romantic trips, dinners, and other gestures.

- Mirroring of your likes and dislikes, making you feel that you have a lot in common.

- Saying "I love you" within weeks of dating. Their 'I love you' doesn't mean 'I love you' the way we understand it; it means 'I love you like I love a car or a cool new toy'.

- Beautiful promises and proclamations, depending on your dreams and needs: *"We were meant for each other," "I feel like you are my soulmate," "I never met anyone like you before ... we have a special connection," "You are the love of my life," "I have been waiting my whole life for a man/woman like you," "We are so similar," "I want to spend the rest of my life with you,"* etc.

Other key psychopathic traits

- Strong sexual appetite – a great time in bed.

- Staring deeply and hypnotically into your eyes, or eyes dancing at you. Their unusual eye contact may seem sexy or romantic at this stage.

Expect the following at the manipulation/devaluing stage:

Manipulation and mind games as controlling mechanisms. Psychopaths cannot keep people through love or other genuine means; they can only use manipulation and manufactured dependency to keep targets bonded to them.

- Massive, covert psychological manipulation to wear you down systematically.

- Mind games to make you feel unhinged and anxious.

- The use of threats and an environment of fear to control you.

- Gradual isolation from social supports like friends or family members.

- Gradual undermining of your self-confidence. *The weaker your self-esteem, the less willpower you have to leave and the more control they have over you.*

- Using your weaknesses and twisting your positive traits against you.

- Gaslighting of your environment and reality to keep you off-balance.

Cheating and conning

- Either overtly manipulating and draining you for money through bank account transfers, maxing out your credit, signing loans, and so on, or covertly stealing your money, forging signatures, and engaging in other activities behind your back. *If overt, they may promise to pay you back, but the fulfillments won't materialize.*

- Cheating with other men or women, either done in front of you or done behind your back, perhaps with a double life on Internet sites and forums.

Calculated hot and cold behavior

- Making you feel desperate for just an ounce of affection and kindness from them, which makes you willing to push your moral boundaries further and lower for their approval.

- Engaging in petty and mean-spirited ways of punishing you (e.g. silent treatments) if you assert your needs or refuse to bend to their will.

- Throwing bones of charm, love, and affection at pivotal moments to string you along and create doubt that you are being abused.

- An overall feeling that nothing you do will ever be good enough and it's your fault the relationship has faltered.

Brazen machinations

- Capable of making up complete jobs, careers, and other situations to manipulate you into staying, along with all the props and behaviors to go along with the machinations, such as faking going to a job every morning, forged documents and degrees, and faking phone conversations.

Other key psychopathic behaviors

- Words will be used to control. They will not be used for open exchange, mutual understanding, or working things out.

- Underhanded sabotaging actions, deception, and pathological lying will all be engaged in. They will generally say one thing and do another.

- Spying, recording, and videotaping without your knowledge, in order to get all the information under their control.

Expect the following at the discard/abandonment stage:

The psychopath:

- Will not leave your life quietly but with humiliating, degrading, and demeaning drama, the kind of scene that they get off on.

- Will wait for the right moment to dump you to inflict the maximum emotional pain, making sure that they break up with you on their own terms (for power and control).

- Will blame you, making you feel the breakup was due to your behavior issues. Label you as crazy, jealous, and so on. Do everything possible to make you feel totally worthless, inferior, and small.

- Will line up the next target in advance before you are discarded. They will immediately show off the new target and their new happy life on Facebook and through other avenues. *This is to see your reaction and erode your self-esteem.*

- Will, if you remain in contact, instigate a post-breakup 'superiority routine'. They will patronize and talk down to you, giving you advice because they are in a relationship or married, and you are not. *This is to self-confirm that they won this game and asserted their superiority.*

- Will start insidious smear campaigns, spreading malicious gossip around your social circle to demolish your reputation. *This is a pre-emptive strike to silence and isolate you socially in case you start telling others what the psychopath is really like.*

If you leave or discard them before they are ready, they will:

- Win you back, so they can dump you on their terms.

- Create an aura of fear and intimidation to gain control.

- Harass and stalk you for months onward (another manifestation of control).

They don't miss you. They miss controlling you and messing with your mind.

How to Ensure Safety in Dating and Romance

The common outcomes of most psychopath-empath relationships can be traced to two main decisions on the part of the empath:

1. Rushing the relationship.

2. Not doing enough background research on the individual before making big decisions, such as getting married or moving in.

The choice of a serious or long-term partner is one of life's biggest decisions. The people you surround yourself intimately with will influence all aspects of your life. This choice should not be made lightly or impulsively. The wrong choice can be costly. Following involvement, it can take years to rebuild your emotional stability, self-esteem, finances, and life.

Hence, the most important things to remember are **research** and **going slow**.

If you do both, your chances of extricating yourself safely from a potentially unwise situation are much higher.

Below, we will logically dissect the ways in which psychopaths and manipulators lure and enlist their prey. We will then systematically recommend effective countermeasures.

The Five Factors of Psychopathic Entrapment

Predatory individuals depend on five factors to lure someone into a romance web.

For quick reference, the predator's methods and our countermeasures are summarized in the chart on the following page and expanded later.

To the predator, **all five factors are absolute necessities** to achieve their aims. For the targets, those are vulnerabilities that you should protect against and block, in order to minimize risk for you.

Although it is not essential to adopt all of them while dating, the more countermeasures you do adopt, the lower your risk of making an unwise choice becomes.

All five factors of entrapment possess ample red flags and warning signs. The wise individual will notice the warning signs, slow down, do their research, and avoid progressing to the next stage of involvement.

Factor	Description	Common Psychopath MO	Countermeasures to Keep You Safe
1.	Access	Lacks stable social networks for normal introductions. Frequently preys online.	Date people whose background you are familiar with in real life. If possible, try friendship first.
2.	Image	A master of impression management. Spends most effort on attractive image.	Value internal character, not appearances or image.
3.	Charm and Grooming	Wears down your defenses with rapid grooming: extreme charm, smoothness, love bombing or pity plays.	Let someone's true nature unfold in time. Suspect the following if they just met you: • Excessive charm and flattery • Feelings of "too good to be true" • Pity plays • Claims of deep emotional connection
4.	Information Imbalance	Draws out information from you for mirroring, supply assessment, and future leverage to be used against you.	Delay full self-disclosure before trust is earned. Listen twice as much as you talk. Note red flags in answers.
5.	Speed	Rushes the relationship. Wants to move in or marry you quickly.	Put brakes on whirlwind romance. Execute full background research and logical prerequisites before big decisions.

Factor 1 - Access

Psychopaths may have many associates and superficial relationships, but most have no real friends (due to the inability to form warm, close personal bonds). This means that in real life they lack a stable social network.

They do not possess the genuine, long-term, and intimate social connections to meet people like you in more natural circumstances, such as through good friends of friends, and friends of family. These are contexts in which similarities in values, social milieu, and socio-economic level are already established.

Consequently, these predators prey online and in seemingly serendipitous circumstances where *natural social bridges* aren't required. The digital era is the psychopath's dream. It's easier than ever to reinvent yourself through new profiles and online platforms, using technological capability to present an artificial image, scaled to impress masses of strangers.

Your defense countermeasures

How and where one meets candidates for a romantic relationship is a personal choice. However, to reduce risk:

1. Date people whose background you are familiar with within your social network, where there are already commonalities of values and unofficial references (in terms of friends you know in common). This shuts out people with questionable histories.

2. If you want to date online, the first thing you have to remember when meeting someone is to do your research. Do not immediately assume that an impressive profile,

photos, and facts are true. Always verify and filter people independently before you agree to meet them in person.

3. Initially, always meet your date in public and don't allow them to come to your home until you have known them for a while. Don't let anyone manipulate or pressure you to your place for seemingly innocuous reasons, such as using the bathroom or having a quick drink. You never know what might happen.

4. If at all possible, go slow and be friends first, in order to get to know someone's character in relaxed environments. Psychopaths typically have very little interest in friendship. Friendship allows you to evaluate who a person truly is in an environment without the pressures of winning over, impressing someone, or putting on the exaggerated airs and performances associated with dating. If someone cannot be a worthy friend, they won't be able to handle the challenging and more invested relationship of romance.

Factor 2 - Image

Psychopaths' self-images are defined by visible signs of success, power, and prestige. They expend the most amount of their energy on this compelling, attractive image. Consequently, everything they have will be on the surface.

Being masters of impression management, they will use many props (including people) to convey this false image. You can expect smooth manners, presentation, the right car, name-dropping, the right clothing, a lot of time spent on looks, questionable credentials designed to impress, association with popular and famous people – basically whatever props are required for the current situation.

Since no effort is exerted to developing what's inside, you will eventually find everything underneath is completely lacking. Their seemingly good judgment and social morals are only word deep.

Your defense countermeasures

The best defense mechanism against being swayed by an artificial image is using a different value system. Image can be faked. If you only care about looks and image, you are setting yourself up for inevitable disappointment.

Look beyond the surface. **Be impressed with internal character**. Many people of true wealth and integrity are discreet, down-to-earth, and not showy. It takes a while to see their real value.

Instead of going for perfection according to a set of societal standards, look for authenticity and genuineness.

Factor 3 - Charm and Grooming

Predators are frequently unbelievably charming. The initial euphoria includes a 'love bombing' of compliments, attention, perfect lines, charm, gifts, and stories that rouse your sympathies. But make no mistake, the agenda is sinister, and the ultimate goal is subversive control.

Be aware that **almost all psychopaths** start with mirroring and promises of eternal love, friendship, or devotion.

Their goal is to:

1. Establish instant emotional intimacy and bonding.

2. Wear down your natural defenses.

3. Groom you so that you eventually become dependent on their positive reinforcements.

Your defense countermeasures

Instead of being blinded by how someone makes you *feel*, pay equal attention to what type of person they are overall.

Be suspicious if you experience the following with someone you just met:

- Excessive charm and flattery

- A feeling of being 'too good to be true'

- Sob stories or pity plays for your sympathy

- Claiming to feel immediate emotional connection with you, or agreeing with every opinion you have

Even in situations where people do feel instant, soul-mate-type emotions, those who truly value and respect the relationship will take things slowly (and wait until the relationship is on solid ground) before communicating such declarations. Waiting is a sign of respect for the relationship. It allows enough time to build the foundations of trust, respect, communication, and underlying friendship, so that it may last. If someone is jumping the gun, you have to wonder what their real motives are.

Factor 4 - Information Imbalance

This step is critical for predators to tailor their 'résumé' to the job. The more they know about you, the more they can mirror and tailor themselves to win you. They will ask a lot of questions to get information out of you, under the guise of strong interest, whereas their own disclosures are vague, fake (designed to hook you in but consisting of made-up stories and personas), or inconsistent.

Their goal here is threefold:

1. Looking for vulnerabilities to hook you in, to make themselves indispensable to you in order to encourage dependency.

2. Assessing what can be gotten out of you to exploit.

3. Obtaining information to use against you later on, for example, in case you wish to leave before they are done with you.

Your defense countermeasures

While communication is essential in getting to know people, many individuals have the habit of disclosing too much too soon to people they don't know well, just because someone gave them a little attention.

Instead:

1. Turn the tables and ask open-ended and detailed questions on your side. Try to listen twice as much as you talk.

2. At the early stage, have the discretion to hold back from sensitive topics, such as your finances, relationship failures, your ideal man or woman, family history, insecurities, and so on, until more trust is built and developed. **Don't give anyone enough information to become your dream partner.**

3. Pay attention to what the other party discloses. Use what they tell you to decide whether to continue or to keep your distance.

4. Monitor potential red flags and lack of substantiated details. When you *don't* disclose your position on a matter, is the other person vague about themselves? Are they always in agreement with you instead of having real opinions? When you ask detailed questions, are there holes, discrepancies, or not enough details in their story?

5. Lastly, verify critical information at your end, particularly if you start to feel more serious about the person. You can execute a background check independently. There are many options on the market today, typically charging a small fee. You can also ask the same questions in different situations, or ask for more details, and see if the versions of the story add up.

Factor 5 - Speed

Psychopaths and emotional predators rush relationships and emotional intimacy. They orchestrate whirlwind romances of breathtaking excitement so that you are not able to think clearly. Often, they want to move in with you or marry you quickly within a short time of meeting you. What they are really after is something very specific *from you*. They are playing against time. If they don't move fast, their true natures may show.

Your defense countermeasures

Whirlwind romances are great fodder for storybooks and movies – but in real life, they should be viewed cautiously. When combined with big, hasty decisions like marriage, they often lead to disastrous results, as well as a lot of regret whilst untangling the serious consequences in the aftermath.

The very first thing to remember is to put the brakes on **any whirlwind romance** and insist on going at a pace that is comfortable for you. Allow yourself the time to see and evaluate the person in many situations. Then follow with the tips below:

1. A good way to test someone is to slow down and carefully observe how the person acts. If they respond by moving in closer, regardless of what you explicitly said you needed, they are only interested in their own agenda (which could be as simple as alleviating their sense of impending rejection – or something more dangerous).

   This is an initial red flag you shouldn't ignore. They are not respecting your boundaries or caring about your well-being. Chasing you at this point isn't a compliment or a testament to how attractive you are, it is about prioritizing **their needs and not yours.**

2. Remember that trust is earned. No one is entitled to it before they have earned it. If someone pressures or criticizes you to gain blind trust, this is a red flag and violation of your rights. Alternatively, if you want to build a relationship, make trust and patience your bricks and mortar. Strong emotions are not enough on their own. As we know now, emotions can often be manipulated.

3. In big decisions such as marriage, moving in, or loaning financial support, create a list of logical prerequisites to check off in order to engage your rational and planning side.

   View marriage as a business partnership. You can still build a wonderful future, but you also need to take a practical approach of preventative control. Some rational prerequisites before marriage may include: full background research, evaluating the current ability to openly communicate and compromise, meeting and getting to know each other's families, approval from friends, financial transparency on both sides, and potentially a prenuptial agreement in case of divorce.

Just an ounce of rational planning minimizes the risk of exploitive predators. Due to outcome clarity and the experience of teamwork, these precautions actually help the success of solid partnerships.

4. In particular for romantic relationships, a common mistake is to rush into marriage without understanding or getting to know your partner's family and family dynamics. This is a mistake. These are people who have known this person their whole life, which makes them an extremely valuable source of information on what they are really like.

You should take a quietly observational and evaluative approach, bearing in mind such questions as: How does the person speak about their own family? Are they willing to introduce you, or do they avoid talking about it? What is the person's family like? How do they get on? What does the family say about the person, and vice versa?

If your partner's family are deceased or otherwise unavailable, research and verify this independently. Predators make up convenient fabrications to evoke sympathy and to cover their tracks.

5. At any time, if your rational boundaries are disrespected – if your partner pressures you to give up your logical reservations and concerns with accusations, threats, or

any behavior other than respect and thoughtful consideration – this is a giant red flag.

Don't let your sentimentality cloud the *underlying disregard* for your best interest.

Disrespect and boundary-pushing behavior only gets worse, not better.

You either leave now, when there is less invested, or leave later with costlier consequences.

In closing this section, it may be wise to change your own world view.

Know that it is much better to be single, happy, and in control of your life, than coupled with a disordered individual; and having your entire life controlled, drained, or destroyed by someone who does not have your best interest at heart.

Understanding Intimate Friendship as the Baseline for Any Successful Relationship

"Loving people live in a loving world. Hostile people live in a hostile world. Same world."

– Wayne Dyer

Many relationship experts believe that friendship is the foundation in which the best relationships grow. To this, we add the following rule:

The ability to maintain intimate friendships also signifies one's ability to maintain a satisfying romantic relationship.

The main reasons are **equality** and **power balance**.

The underlying tenet of a fulfilling romantic relationship is the ability to treat people as equals. Close friendships are inherently based on equality. If a person has no close friends, it is likely that they never learned how to relate to other individuals on an equal basis. They won't be able to have an equal relationship on any level, romantic or otherwise.

Through the experience of forming genuine, close friendships, one also practices, develops, and perfects the following six relating skills:

1. Mutual empathy and caring.

2. Ability to have heart-to-heart chats and to openly communicate.

3. Ability to like, understand, and accept someone as is, the good and the bad.

4. Capacity to uphold commitments, promises, and social obligations.

5. Ability to compromise for mutually satisfying outcomes.

6. Ability to look beyond self-interest for the benefit of the relationship.

The relating skills above are also essential foundations for a successful romantic relationship.

In romantic relationships, you spend more time together. With two different personalities and interests interweaving as one, more psychological irritation and more joint challenges can result.

If someone has failed to develop relating skills through intimate friendships as a baseline, how could they possibly handle the challenging demands of a relationship?

Within a long-term timespan, these related inadequacies reveal themselves and culminate in the inevitable collapse of relationships.

You can effectively use genuine, close friendships as a barometer to judge whether someone possesses the *relating skills* necessary for satisfactory relationships.

The Dominance Bond versus Equality and the Power Balance

"For me there are only two kinds of women, goddesses and doormats."

– Pablo Picasso

Psychopaths relate to other people with a dominance bond and/or a superficial persona. They do not have friendships based on equality, intimacy, and a fair power balance. They can engage in superficial relationships that can be mistaken for friendship when seen from a distance – but make sure you look closer at the inherent power balance and emotional attachment.

Their typical relationships are with:

- Targets under their control

- Superficial acquaintances, activity partners, and hang-out buddies, only familiar with their outward persona

- Inferior sidekicks

- Groupies and followers to lead and manipulate

- Accomplices and relationships of mutual utility

If you get romantically involved with a man or woman who only seems to engage in the above relationships, they will treat you the same way as they treat all others, within the entire spectrum of their relating capacity, perhaps as a groupie or follower to lead and manipulate, or someone to maneuver into a weaker position for control, but always in terms of the same dominance bond – not with you, but over you.

With the extreme psychopath, many people are flabbergasted at illogical things their partners do – leading to frustrating and futile attempts in counseling, discussions, fights, and contracts.

To gain clarity, one must understand that the psychopathic instinct for the dominance bond means they have neither the *capacity* nor the *real intent* to work anything out, and

they are incapable of having a nice relationship the way most of us understand it.

If your expectations of a romantic relationship are based on equality, open communication, and mutual emotional support, getting involved with such an individual inevitably leads to disappointment, even devastation.

Using the Friendship Rule in Dating

Using this rule in dating, it is wise to pay close attention to the following:

1. **Existing capacity for equality and power balance.** Consider whether the person in question has real long-term friends, people they are truly close to. How do they treat people they consider their close friends? And, probing beneath the surface, what is the power balance and inner dynamic of those relationships?

2. **Capacity for building a steady and strong foundation with you.** Go slow and be friends first. Observe them in various situations before taking the relationship to the next level. If someone lacks the ability to uphold the tenets of friendship (respect, empathy, trust, a fair power balance), they will be a disastrous relationship candidate.

A healthy and satisfying relationship is comprised of respect, trust, underlying friendship, and similar values. These truths will always stand the test of time.

Methods of Operation in Divorce and Custody Battles

The closer you get to a psychopath and the longer you are involved with them, the more damage it will cause to your life and mental health. In an open battle with a psychopath (for example, in trying to leave them), they will employ every tactic in their arsenal to make your life hell.

If you are caught in an open divorce or custody battle with a psychopath, it will be an ugly, long, uphill battle.

Expect the following:

Leverage and destruction

They will bring out all the weaknesses and information they know about you as leverage in warfare.

- They *will* use the kids against you.

- Their actions will be calculated to inflict the maximum emotional damage.

- They will spread insidious rumors and gossip to trigger an emotional reaction.

- Whatever they did to you in the relationship, they will now make you seem like the aggressor, predator, and themselves the victim. This is a consistent pattern to the game they play. Expect:

  - Pre-emptive protective orders against *you*, making you seem like the abuser.

  - Spreading of lies to the legal system and your social network to make *you* look like the bad guy.

- – Allegations involving drugs, prostitution, or other defamation in order to destroy your career or reputation – basically anything you value or worked hard for.
- They will leak sensitive, personal information that could harm you (such as sex tapes or negative things you said about others).
- They will use identity theft, using your personal information, such as your social security number, for fraud. This is designed to psychologically unbalance you, as well as cause financial harm.

Mind games to create psychological and emotional torment

- Threats, intimidation, and spreading of fear, veiled or overt, to attack your weaknesses. The more you care about something, the more they will threaten it and try to destroy it.

- Heartfelt letters, apologies, and solicitations of prior love, designed to trigger emotions, confuse, and weaken resolves (alternating with the threats and intimidation).

- Pity plays for your sympathy, painting themselves as the victim (again, in-between the threats and intimidation).

- Staging or faking events to elicit sympathy, drama, and confusion, such as faking illness, accidents, or even faking suicide attempts.

Other behaviors

- Spying, snooping, stalking, harassing behavior.

- A prolonged battle just to drain you financially and emotionally.

They will be motivated by:

- Money (property, long-term spousal support, your checking, savings, and retirement accounts)
- Control
- Winning this game of destroying you and causing you harm
- Revenge against you for discarding them

They won't be bothered by:

- Moral codes – there are no restrictions
- Emotional obligation, alleged loyalty, or remorse – though they play your emotions to get what they want, they are incapable of emotional obligation
- Any harm they cause to you – you were just an object and a means to an end
- Any harm they cause to their children – they are just pawns in the game

Psychopaths often succeed in open conflict with an empath due to reliance on three factors:

1. Your emotions, sympathies, compassion, or pangs of past love: these sentiments make one soft and hesitant to fight back, while the psychopath is planning their moves from a cold and unsentimental standpoint. They manipulate your emotions, and hence your behaviors.

2. Your moral integrity: they depend on you to fight fair and play nice.

3. Your openness: they depend on you to be honest, open, and transparent. Most people give themselves away easily enough for a psychopath to anticipate their next moves.

With a psychopath, openness does you no favors – especially not open defiance. Your weapon is stealth, keeping everything secret, while playing and acting a completely different front on the surface. Lure them into a false sense of security. You need a thorough escape plan, and you need to think outside the box. The key is to adjust your expectations secretly.

In most cases, if you fight them openly and through the normal system, you will lose. You will lose more than just money, but your health and psychological well-being will be battered further by a prolonged legal battle, most likely leading to a desperate decision just to end it. Many lawyers in the legal battle could be psychopaths themselves!

Your moral codes, not wishing to sink to their levels, naivety, inexperience of working the system, current human state of emotion (anger, remorse, sympathy) will be absolutely no match for their unrestricted tactics, psychological battering, a lifetime of deceit, lack of emotion, and lack of guilt.

To get an idea and to prepare for what you are up against, I recommend the book *Splitting: Protecting Yourself While Divorcing Someone with Borderline or Narcissistic Personality Disorder* by Bill Eddy and Randi Kreger. The book is solely focused on legal patterns of the two aforementioned disorders, which are generally considered as less dangerous than psychopaths. We can infer from there how further depraved a genuine psychopath may sink to.

Here are questions that may help as you devise an escape plan:

1. Think about how companies and managers get 'problem employees' to leave without causing lawsuits. What tactics can you learn to get the psychopath to leave on their own?

2. Think of what they want from you, the benefits they glean from you – how do you engineer a situation that makes those benefits gradually disappear, through no obvious fault of your own?

3. What are they like experience-wise and behaviorally? Only you can answer this question. Are they physically violent? Do they have extensive military experience in killing? Do they have the means and capability to drug or poison you? Would they gain insurance money if you were removed? Would they hire a hit man to eliminate you? Can they tamper with your vehicle? These questions may sound far-fetched, but it's important to understand that you are nothing but an object to them. The risk is real. Depending on what you know, as well as your gut instinct, you should remove yourself from their vicinity as soon as possible so that they have no physical access to you, or the means to keep tabs on your schedule. Your safety should be your number one priority.

Chapter 3
How to Defend Yourself
Once and For All

"If you know the enemy and know yourself, you need not fear the results of a hundred battles. If you know yourself but not the enemy, for every victory gained you will also suffer a defeat. If in ignorance of both of your enemy and yourself, you are certain to be in peril."

– Sun Tzu, The Art of War

In this chapter, we will systematically analyze the psychopath's advantages, so as to render them ineffective, defend against them mentally, review their weaknesses, and build behavioral walls against them.

There are two points to keep in mind:

1. The recommendations in the chapter are intended for use with manipulative people and environments; they are not given as advice for how to live all aspects of your life. Honesty, kindness, love, and trust are what makes life enriching and worth living. **Do** reserve those wonderful qualities for those in your life who are deserving of them.

2. Remember, when faced with a psychopath, you are dealing with someone for whom deception is second nature. Being honest, genuine, and nice will not work. Those are counterproductive behaviors that open yourself up to exploitation and defeat. If you try to deal with a psychopath in an ethical manner, you will be in for a shock. You might as well concede defeat or yield to exploitation if

planning to negotiate and bargain with a psychopathic, or otherwise deceptive individual, as though with an honest, genuine, altruistic person. Don't take risks by following 'proper' protocol. To defend against these types, you must engage in *protective counter-deception.*

How Do You Protect or Defend Yourself When in the Company of a Psychopath?

For everyday purposes, a psychopath succeeds in luring, manipulating, and hurting targets due to reliance on five factors:

1. **Camouflage and trust** – The #1 reason a psychopath succeeds is due to the majority of people not being aware of their true, deceitful natures. Society believes that all people have some good in them and most empaths are entirely unprepared for other tactics. It's far easier to manipulate unsuspecting, naive people who are taught to be good and tend to trust appearances, so the psychopath always presents an authentic, caring, upstanding image, totally different than what's underneath.

2. **The openness of others** – Most people are taught that regular and thorough communication is a positive trait. Personal information, gossip, and plans are shared without restraint. The psychopath is easily able to collect information about you during an assessment stage to build a mental picture of you, and later to use what they know to control, manipulate, and threaten.

3. **Preying on your weaknesses and vulnerabilities** – Because they are unemotional, they can easily detect a target's vulnerabilities. Having no conscience, any knowledge of your weakness is an opportunity for domination and control.

4. **Creating fear** – There are two primary emotions in life: love and fear. They use the machinations of love to lure someone into their web. Fear is their chief weapon when

they want to silence, intimidate, or control you for their own ends.

5. **People's showiness** – This is related to the openness mentioned above. In our culture, we are often quick to show off what we have and to brag about our accomplishments or achievements. This tendency for display creates targets for the psychopath to use or sabotage.

If you suspect someone you know is a psychopath and you have to deal with them, execute the following. For the long term, it's safest to have no relationship with them.

1. **Know exactly what you are dealing with.** This is a top priority. You can't protect yourself if you have any illusions or lingering sympathies. **Review the identifying list and the reminder list for NCEA.** It may take a while to sink in, but once you accept that these people exist everywhere, they can never fool you again. Remember not to reveal your inner knowledge.

2. **Keep them at a perpetual information deficit.** Don't reveal anything personal that can be used against you. Never tell the person in question what type of support system you have. Don't introduce them to any of your social circles. **And most importantly, don't reveal any important plans until they are already complete.**

3. **Never reveal weaknesses.** One option is to feed completely false knowledge about weaknesses. Exploiting people's emotional buttons and provoking reactions is a primary weapon. **Never reveal your true emotions. Act like Mr. Spock around them** – always unemotional and in control of yourself, pleasant and robotic.

4. **Never show fear.** Fake it if you need to.

5. **Hide what they want and control your impulse to show off and brag.** This goes against our natural impulse to show off. If you have anything they may want – money, connections, prestige – hide it when you are around them. They are covetous and, due to jealousy, will ruthlessly exploit or sabotage. Figure out what they are after and hide it. If it's too late to hide it, find an excuse – in an unemotional, non-confrontational way – not to be able to provide it.

If they are after your money, create the impression you don't have a lot of money anymore – that you lost it, that it was stolen. Secure all financial information, as a psychopath may be quite ready to read your bank statements, hack your mail, and hack into accounts behind your back. If they want your connections, try to create the impression you are not well-connected or have fallen out of touch with the friends or colleagues in question. If something nice happens to you – inheritance, award, new boyfriend/girlfriend – keep it from them.

Particularly for women (though also for men), understand that a psychopath may see you as a supply for sex and will fully exploit the opportunity if the situation presents itself. No social constraints – friendship, family, the workplace, underage minors, mentor/teacher relationships – are taboo. To protect yourself, it would be wise to never be with them alone, or to accept any drinks from them if you can avoid it.

How to Recondition and Discipline *Your* Thought Process

Psychopaths and manipulative characters have many weapons in their arsenal to lower your defenses. Our natural impulse from years of social conditioning is to trust immediately, to be open and candid.

Without strategic and disciplined mental defenses, **no one** can be immune to the repeated onslaughts of false fronts, false personas, and false promises, combined with pushy, aggressive behavior. You will get sucked in somehow, doubt yourself, and end up feeling crazy or hurt.

With those individuals, we need to switch 180 degrees in the way we *think* about them. This is more important than changing our behavior. It's reconditioning and disciplining the mind to construct the proper defense mechanisms to protect against their mind games. The mental tactics below increase your defenses to impenetrable levels.

Once you suspect someone is a psychopath, mentally:

1. **Treat everything they say as a lie, unless proven true.** Typically, we treat everything as true unless proven false. With these individuals, you need to train yourself to think exactly the opposite, regardless of how kind the surface persona seems or how authentically they speak. Practice assuming everything is a lie and not listening to anything they say; instead, look at what they do. Independently research any important facts coming from them, and never indicate that you are on your guard.

2. **Question all motives, whether they are perceived as good or bad.** If the individual opens or joins a charity, question their motives. If they kiss a baby in a photo-op

or adopt a puppy, question their real motives. If they apologize and are especially nice to you, *definitely* question their motives. If they are asking you to do **anything** for sentimental reasons, a 'one last time,' a 'forgiveness for past wrongs,' making beautiful promises, be very suspicious. This is a play on your emotions – a classic psychopath move, a red flag which indicates that they are using a manipulation tactic for a secret agenda. The more moving and touching the emotional play, the more seriously you should take the underlying threat.

3. **Always, always trust your intuition when dealing with them.** Psychopathic individuals are masters of cognitive dissonance – presenting a genuine-seeming appearance that hides their true selves. This is where nature's built-in warning signals come in handy. In Stout's *Thirteen Rules for Dealing with Sociopaths in Everyday Life*, she recommends, "In a contest between your instincts and what is implied by the role a person has taken on – educator, doctor, leader, animal lover, humanist, parent – go with your instincts."[1] Again, in that crucial battle between your intuition and a role that person is taking on (such as world's best parent and family person, an older and helpful mentor, a feminist, an apologetic and guilt-ridden ex-partner, a police officer), go with your intuition no matter **what** anyone else says, how appealing their image is, or how many others admire them.

4. **If they promise you something you really want, take this up as a silent challenge to achieve it yourself without their help, involvement, or knowledge.**

Promises and bribery that hit the mark can be a powerful manipulation tactic. Even when we know the promise-maker cannot be trusted, the possibility of getting something we would really love to have appeals to our natural greed and the hope to see our wishes come true. There is always that little voice in the back of our head that says, *"Maybe they can help me attain this; maybe there is a slim glimmer of hope."* And thus, you play into a web of dependency, with emotional investment and expectations set.

The influence is subtle, and the target may remain unconscious of the effects. However, any mental or emotional investment, no matter how small or fleeting, can lead to disappointment, and emotional and psychological hurt when nothing materializes. This is precisely the reason psychopaths frequently play these types of psychological games with others. **They dangle, string you along, push those buttons, make you feel invested, create expectations and hope, and then shatter them.**

To protect yourself from falling into a manufactured state of dependency, ask instead: *How do I obtain this end goal myself without any help or involvement from them?* Start brainstorming, start planning, start taking action.

This way, instead of coming out as the potential loser from their manipulation tactics, you will come out as the winner no matter what they do. You will be asking the right questions and putting yourself on the path to **self-sufficiency and self-reliance**.

As a side note, never reveal your new plan, goals, or thoughts to the person in question. If you do, a deceptive individual will do all they can to sabotage them.

5. **Detach by viewing their machinations as entertainment.** Focusing on your moral outrage creates anger and

may emotionally cloud your ability for rational planning. It may even affect your mood and behavior around them.

You will never change them. Thus, a tactic must be employed to regain rationality *for you*. This does not mean you tolerate, agree, or join in with their behavior. When you are rational, you can focus on productive endeavors in your life and calmly execute plans to completion.

To detach from the situation and reinforce rationality, envision them now as a ball of buffoonery.

- Are they crusading for a social cause? Laugh secretly and be amused that they learned a new trick to con others. They are probably creating a new persona for a new scam with a new social network.

- Are they profusely apologizing and making x, y, and z promises? Laugh secretly. They probably want something from you – a new con for a fresh game, small-minded and absurd.

This method removes expectations, which is the prerequisite to emotional hurt.

When you secretly laugh at them while presenting a neutral front, detaching and discarding them from your life will become easy. This does not mean you get any closer to the psychopath. Social and physical boundaries, or a complete avoidance, must be enforced for your own safety.

How to Deflect a Psychopath to Other Targets

In the long term, the only safe method to avoid the effects a psychopath may have on you is to keep such people out of your life. Manipulative individuals will employ different tactics to worm their way into your trust. Keeping them in your life is a draining, uphill battle. It means 24/7 caution, alertness, and energy that can best be applied elsewhere.

However, for situations where you have to deal with them, the following steps should repel psychopaths from trying to handle you.

Step 1 - Erect Rock-solid Boundaries

This step is absolutely the most important.

Most people that attract or fall into the web of a psychopath have blurry or relaxed boundaries. They are typically empathetic people who need to merge or blend in with others, losing themselves in another's identity or emotion.

Typically, the empath doesn't know what a boundary is – and the psychopath has never met a boundary he or she didn't cross.

Here are two rules to remember:

1. **One way to recognize predatory abusers is that they always push and test boundaries.** A person who isn't abusive per se, but still has a secret and dangerous agenda, will also push boundaries.

2. **Predators use slippery slopes to lure you in.** How does this work? They will start with a small boundary violation, something so subtle and innocuous that it causes

doubt in your mind, making you wonder if you are just over-thinking it. If you don't respond, then they aim bigger and go in for the kill.

To completely repel them, immediately respond to a boundary violation with stricter boundaries.

For example, if they are pushing too close to your personal space and making you uncomfortable, immediately detach, and calmly and politely say you prefer to have your personal space at all times. Then firmly maintain a certain distance when speaking to them.

Would you lose some people's friendship this way? Maybe. But you will likely find that those who are worth getting to know, and have your best interests at heart, will respect your boundaries after the fact.

And if they act inappropriately, harass, ignore you, push further, make you feel guilty, make fun of you, or act petty or extra-offended? Well, now you know exactly who to stay the hell away from.

Step 2 - Be Boring – Channel the Grey Rock Method

Psychopaths want their ego, their need for drama, excitement, and admiration, satisfied. It doesn't matter if it's a positive or negative reaction; they live to know they have power over someone's emotions. It's pure entertainment for them.

To repel them, don't give them any emotion, interest, or energy that will satisfy them. Don't argue with them or show any excitement. Instead, be completely boring and flat-toned, and only talk about the most tedious, boring things in detail.

To fully execute this method, you may want to practice a social mask to wear in circumstances such as this. Practice a mask of few facial expressions, robotic disinterest, boring responses, stoic emotions, and slow, monotonous talk – much like a grey rock that is unnoticed and blends in with the environment. Reserve your natural, expressive self with those you trust.

Psychopaths are easily bored and will view chasing you as an unsatisfying, boring pursuit. They will soon put their energies elsewhere – exactly where you want them.

Step 3 - Never Make Instant Decisions When They Are Around

Truly empathic people soak up others' emotions and energy easily, and sometimes even thoughts. They are prone to persuasion and are affected by heightened suggestibility and subtly manipulative tactics from unscrupulous individuals.

To avoid absorbing moods and energies that are not your own, you need to be sufficiently distanced from pressuring environments and people.

Practice the firm habit to **always** take time out to think alone. And, without exception, make decisions when you are alone, in your own energy. Never make any instant decisions around a psychopath. To do this, you will need to buy time (see #4).

There are two benefits to this:

1. The more you practice making decisions by getting in touch with your own energy and inner needs, the more confidence you will build in trusting yourself, and the

happier you will become by shielding out negative and time-wasting situations. It's a positive, win-win cycle.

2. You will be seen as someone who's harder to crack. If you are also seen as boring, with strict boundaries, and little to offer, a psychopath will move on to someone who's an easier target.

Step 4 - Use and Practice 'Go Nowhere' Answers

In situations when the individual is extremely pushy, practice a variety of 'go nowhere', circular answers, such as:

I'll think about it.

Perhaps later, we'll see.

Maybe.

You can use simple lines or be as convoluted as you want. The important thing is not to show emotion; don't ever say yes or give any specifics, but don't overtly reject or offend them either. Obfuscate in an emotionless, polite manner.

Use whatever 'go nowhere' answers you need to buy time, don't allow them to pin you down, and then execute actions to slip away.

Step 5 - Never Be in Their Debt – Not Even a Free Drink

In life, sooner or later, we realize nothing is ever really free.

With a predator, this is even more the case, as their strategies are to dangle favors in front of you in order to unconsciously wear down your defenses and gain a much bigger return down the road.

A psychopath wants control and power. Whatever favors are presented initially will be used to control you for a secret agenda. You will pay the cost sooner or later. What they want from you is always grossly unequal to what was originally offered.

Adopt the rule of **never** accepting anything from them – no free drinks, no free car rides, no free lunches. Don't give in to pressure, guilt, or words that seem extremely generous or kind. If you need help, find someone you trust to help you instead. Insist on paying for yourself. If you accidentally became indebted to them, immediately even out the debt *on your terms* so they have zero control over you.

The benefit of enacting this rock-solid rule is that it further fortifies your wall of boundaries so that it becomes impenetrable against those who wish to exploit you.

How Do You Influence a Psychopath?

Based on what we know about psychopathic personalities, we can divide recommendations into three categories: short-term, long-term, and entanglements that may be undesirable, but are forced by necessity.

Short-term

In the short-term, you may be able to get psychopathic individuals to play ball by offering a short-term reward that fits into their self-interest.

Remember that a psychopath is incapable of exertion for others' welfare. All their actions, under any guise, represent investments made to satisfy their immediate needs and desires.

To influence the psychopath, you need to correctly identify their motivation, as they will always act in their own self-interest. You also need to provide immediate rewards, because they are incapable of long-term thinking.

Long-term

For the long-term, revealing private or sensitive information, keeping the psychopath around or trusting them, places you and important parts of your life at risk.

In those times, remember that in any social situation, whether you meet them at work, in romance, family relationships, or in landlord/tenant situations, for them it is always a game of control and domination. Any help you give to psychopaths will always be repaid to you by treachery.

These types operate with the dominance bond as their fundamental nature. Their tools are betrayal, backstabbing, and trickery.

You need to abandon the illusion that there can be peaceful coexistence or mutual understanding, as you would expect with normal individuals who possess a conscience, the capacity for loyalty, and the ability to uphold promises and agreements.

Unavoidable situations

Lastly, for unavoidable situations where you must bargain with psychopaths, there is another method that can be effective in dealing with them.

Keep in mind that when dealing with what we might call 'extreme' individuals, there is no easy solution. There is no warm, fuzzy, or fast conclusion; and those looking for it need to give up the fantasy that it exists. There will be a cost in effort, time, or material benefits regardless of the situation. Hence, we mention this part last, and we recommend the **prevention** and **no contact** method first and foremost.

In his book, *In Sheep's Clothing*, George Simon was the first to mention win-win as a method to deal with covert aggressives.[2] This concept is more deeply explored and expanded here.

The following theory provides a foundation for the general underlying idea, which can then be used and applied to many situations, big and small. These are key concepts, worth reading through a few times in order to grasp their logic and rationale, and to aid consideration of their applicability to different situations.

In any given negotiation between two parties, there are four outcomes:

PERSON A

	Win	Lose
Win (PERSON B)	**1** A: Win B: Win	**2** A: Lose B: Win
Lose (PERSON B)	**3** A: Win B: Lose	**4** A: Lose B: Lose

1. **The first option is win-win.** You gain something, and the other party also gains something. Typically, this outcome is achieved between two individuals who have the capacity to brainstorm together for mutual solutions. Trust is important in this context because it allows both parties to probe and divulge their real needs cooperatively. Often the underlying needs of each individual can both be served by a brand new, creative solution. Thus, both parties win.

2. **The second option is lose-win.** One person wins, and the other person loses. Person B here wins at the expense of Person A.

3. **The third option is win-lose.** The same as above, but with switched roles. Person A here wins at the expense of Person B.

4. **The last option is lose-lose.** Both parties are damaged, and both lose something. This typically occurs in stalemates for one reason or another; usually a lack of trust,

too much pride or stubbornness, vindictiveness, or personality and value conflicts.

Why Win-Win is the Best Outcome

In general, the win-win scenario is the best solution, for normal individuals and, in this case, with psychopaths as well.

Assigning Person A to be the psychopath in the following charts, we can discuss each of the quadrants and outcome scenarios in turn.

PERSON A = PSYCHOPATH

	Win	Lose
Win	**1** A: Win B: Win	**2** A: Lose B: Win
Lose	**3** A: Win B: Lose	**4** A: Lose B: Lose

PERSON B

Quadrant 2: Psychopath loses, you win

PERSON A = PSYCHOPATH

	Win	Lose
Win	**1** A: Win B: Win	**2** A: Lose B: Win
Lose	**3** A: Win B: Lose	**4** A: Lose B: Lose

PERSON B

The second quadrant (Psychopath loses, Person B wins) is actually not an option in the vast majority of situations. A psychopath needs to win at all costs. If a psychopath perceives they have lost and you have won, what will naturally happen is an unrelenting, vindictive attempt to regain power and control, and to change the score. Given their low impulse control, sparking this off can be dangerous. This is also the mistake and minefield many empaths run into: **projecting their concept of justice, fairness, and morality** in dealing with normal people on to someone vastly abnormal. Consequently, this quadrant and outcome is shaded out to indicate its unsuitability as an outcome. Realistically, the outcome will backfire.

Quadrant 3: Psychopath wins, you lose

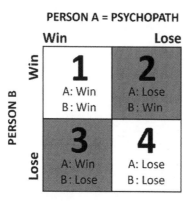

The third quadrant is where you lose, and the psychopath wins. Certainly, this is what *they* want, but it is also what we are here to prevent and defend against. By logic, this is not the outcome we want, so we shade this out.

Quadrant 4: Psychopath loses, you lose

The fourth quadrant is a lose-lose scenario for both parties. Perhaps you may feel vindicated by hurting the psychopath, but you also damage your own interests in the final outcome. This is not the *ideal* final outcome, so we shade this out.

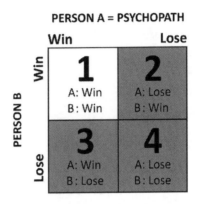

As can be seen, quadrant 1, the win-win, is the ideal outcome. The psychopath feels like they won; hence, reducing the amount of danger for you. You get the benefits you wanted at the start of the scenario without harming anybody else. Most of all, you safeguard what is really important to you.

The Psychopath Constraint

With psychopaths, natural challenges are in play.

First, a psychopath will always come from a competing and deceiving standpoint. Because they expect others to act only out of competitive self-interest, they will always make the pre-emptive competitive strike first – to attack you. If given a choice and they can get away with it, their preferred outcome will always be the third quadrant (Person A: Win, Person B: Lose).

They get what they want at your expense, and they experience the thrill and superiority of conquering and winning over you.

Second, in more natural circumstances, the cooperation required in the win-win situation is alien to a psychopath. One, they don't care or understand the concept of benefiting someone else. Two, the abstract visual of mutual benefit, a bigger picture, or anything larger than their own needs is also alien to them.

So how do you overcome those two constraints?

When external circumstances (either real or orchestrated) make the third quadrant less attractive, more difficult, or just no longer an option, **the psychopath's self-interest is served by switching methods**.

Always focused on self-gain, a much higher percentage will choose the win-win option where they win (they get something of personal value), as compared to the other three remaining options. Remember, their perceiving a win means less danger for you.

To illustrate the theory better, we shade quadrant 2 out once again. In their reality, there is **no way** a psychopath will let you win while they lose. Hence the following visuals are realistically the choices they see.

Now, which one is more attractive?

In both of the outcomes – the win-win or the lose-lose – the psychopath won't give a hoot about what happens to you; but they will care about themselves.

For the first constraint of genuine brainstorming and cooperation, since full trust, transparency, and honesty between two parties is difficult with a character-disordered individual, it's up to you to correctly identify, test, and assess a persuasive motivator for the psychopath, where they can feel like they won.

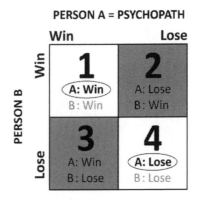

You must know the psychopath fairly well and be creative and insightful enough to figure out a persuasive and motivating benefit for them, to attach to the direction which also benefits you. This benefit is usually one of their personal trigger points, such as money, prestige, power, self-aggrandizement, fame, and so on.

In summary, the underlying principle is to maneuver toward the win-win situation. The strategies, tactics, situation, and circumstance will differ, but the concept is the same – this is the safest outcome that also protects your interests.

Lastly, note that if the psychopath ends up choosing the win-win, you must never depend on their **long-term loyalty** or possess any illusions that a relationship or friendship between you exists.

Avoid giving them any unnecessary information that can be used against you later. Their complaisance is only for this one round, nothing more.

How Do You Defeat a Psychopath?

Below are five summarizations of available methods.

The intent of this guide is not to preach a one-size-fits-all morality. The reader has their own ethics and morality and the reality is that every situation is different.

If you choose to do something beyond NCEA, remember that most psychopaths and deceitful individuals are dangerous, petty, and vengeful. **Always be prudent, consider all consequences, and keep your safety as a number one priority.**

1. The most recommended way of dealing with a psychopath is **NCEA**. Get away from the psychopath permanently as soon as you can. Focus on building your own strong and positive social network, concentrate on the things you love and what makes you the most fulfilled, and forget all about the unworthy. **Any contact** with toxic and unbalanced people produces negative energy and unhappiness in your life.

2. Despite our best efforts to avoid contact, sometimes no contact only escalates matters. The psychopath feels a loss of control and decides to fight to gain it back again.

    If the psychopath is not violent and you are feeling up for the fight, you can use the psychopath's own methods against them. NOTE: *This is not recommended if they have shown any violent tendencies at all in the past.*

    I discovered a terrific blog called *Dating a Sociopath,* by *Positivagirl.*[3] Her post, "Sociopath: How to get even with one" is filled with great advice and, while her message focuses on sociopaths in dating relationships, the same principles can apply to psychopaths in other areas of our lives.

As *Positivagirl* points out, the sociopath (or psychopath) controls you through three avenues:

1. **Generating fear**

2. **Using personal information to manipulate or threaten**

3. **Preying on your weaknesses**

Consider what these three things have in common – power. To a psychopath, any method of gaining the upper hand is fair game.

To completely turn the tables, we must counter with the same tactics they use. Let's separate our counter-warfare into three categories: **action, mindset, and demeanor.**

First, your actions:

- Lie about everything, even inconsequential details about where you've been and what you've done. Be as dishonest as they are. Keep them at an information deficit.

- Feed them false details about your weaknesses and your plans.

- Make big promises, but don't follow through.

- Lure them into a false sense of security.

- Spy on them, monitor them, find something on them to gain the upper hand.

- Be unpredictable, keep them guessing, constantly change.

- Say one thing, then deny you ever said it.

Second, your mindset. To mirror the psychopath's actions successfully, you need to adopt a completely new mindset. No more worries about hurting them or looking for cooperative solutions. You are in a covert guerrilla war, and the below must be your new mentality:

- Whatever they do, you do (within the confines of the law).

- If they threaten you, threaten back.

- If they lie to you, lie back.

- If they deceive or manipulate you, do the same.

Third, your demeaner must not betray any weakness. You must:

- Show no fear.

- Show no emotion.

- Remain calm and pleasant – at least on the surface. Smile, despite what you feel inside.

That's the 1, 2, 3 punch of countering their tactics. Got it?

Using their tactics against them keeps psychopaths on the defensive, creates confusion, and may convince them you are *crazier* than them.

Another positive effect of this tactic is regaining power. You will rebuild the fractured boundaries and restore the stolen energy.

Again, this not recommended if the psychopath is violent. Your safety should be your top priority. If violence is a potential result, pick another method.

3. Covertly investigate, report, or undermine them in a way that keeps you untraceable (for example, report them to the IRS for tax evasion, do a thorough background check on them and mail it anonymously to everyone you know at work). Plan well ahead. Be very, very, careful here and cover your tracks well.

    When dealing with a psychopath, it is **never** a good idea to reveal yourself openly or honestly. You are only opening yourself to be attacked and harmed, covertly or overtly. Your open, perceived victory will be short-lived. Remember, they've almost certainly practiced deceit their entire life. They have no remorse or conscience regarding using the most underhanded and extreme methods if they perceive that they may be in danger, that someone is a threat, or that they can get away with it.

    So, learn from their tactics in reverse. You need to be smart, stealthy, invisible, and effective, giving them no open target to strike back.

4. Give them a small win and get rid of them by pretending to be defeated. If you are accidentally dragged into some deranged game you never agreed to, don't escalate it into a war. Pretend well and let the small defeat go, then execute #1 (NCEA).

    In this situation, ultimately you win because you transcended the pettiness and got your life, energy, and sanity back to achieve great things, while they will always be enmeshed in petty negativity.

    In certain cases, for relationships when your safety is not in danger, it may be best to let them dump you while you secretly catch on to what they are doing. You just need to be one step ahead of them and be a very good actor.

5. Depending on the extremeness of the infraction, if you really want to get even with a psychopath, the key is unrelenting patience and anonymity. You may have to wait years, and you must execute your plan with complete anonymity. By this time, the psychopath will have damaged many others along the way and their pool of victims and enemies (potential suspects) will be numerous. It is not recommended to come out with the truth and reveal yourself openly at any time.

The Weaknesses of Having No Conscience

Every condition has pros and cons. Due to cunning and remorselessness, the psychopath generally operates from a wider range and extremity of underhanded or illegal actions than someone who can experience empathy and conscience. The psychopath also has inherent weaknesses you can use to your advantage in the right situation.

1. Most have **poor impulse control** and **short-term mentalities**. Pissing people off in life collects enemies who patiently wait for a fall, no matter how powerless they seem now. The psychopath is digging their own grave over the long term. Successful scams are based on the winds of luck – and luck eventually changes.

2. The psychopath will **never attract or inspire die-hard loyalty** based on true emotional connection. Most of the time, they may attain the outward semblance of it through manipulation. Other tools in their arsenal are bribery, fear, intimidation, and control. But they have no true loyalty – the loyalty of that rare friend who will fight to the ends of the earth for them. When push comes to shove, no one will sacrifice for them. Love has the power and potential for both sacrifice and loyalty; fear does not. For those the psychopath is bonded to and purports to love, the psychopath is a negative energetic influence – draining and slowly destroying the loved ones closest to them. They undermine any potential support network by rendering those people psychologically and sometimes physically too weak for the type of superhuman feats made possible by a combination of positivity, intelligence, and transcension of fear.

3. In nature one of the biggest known predators of wolves are the wolves themselves, even within the same pack. They attack each other when hungry and when food supplies are low. Similarly, psychopathic accomplices operate by **convenience and utility**, and no other emotional bonds. Short-term and common-interest allies will always betray each other when the right circumstance presents itself. This is an additional weak point in the psychopath's supposedly impermeable armor.

4. The psychopath's background and history is always filled with **skeletons in the closet** waiting for that unusually persistent someone with the right motivation and investigative skills to dig them up. This may yield mines of information and even allies and support in bringing the psychopath down.

5. The psychopath is riddled with **trust issues** and generally full of **paranoia**. The right situation and a very stealthy opponent can turn the psychological games on them.

6. The psychopath is a **loner** with no true social support and no real friends. In fact, they are in the minority, once exposed. Once a situation exposes the false front for what they are, they often have to leave to a new area and create a new persona.

7. No matter how good the camouflage, they can never escape the **instincts and intuition** of other individuals.

Should You Confront the Psychopath with Their Behavior?

Absolutely do not confront the psychopath. They will never change. The only permanent solution is to walk away and refuse any social interaction with them.

Controlling Your Own Tendencies

Here, the empath can become their own worst enemy. You may have to forget everything you thought you knew about how people should treat each other.

When confronted with such abusers, we often have a compulsion to do the following:

1. Tell them about the consequences of their behavior and expect sympathy and understanding of how they have hurt you.

2. Tell them we know what they are or that they are a piece of **** and they should feel guilty for what they have done; expect them to feel bad about themselves and possibly reform.

3. Tell them for the last time we know they are a sociopath/psychopath/narcissist so that we can feel vindicated with the last laugh.

The Consequences

There are three consequences of attempting to work things out with someone who lacks empathy:

1. The more you attempt to talk through things or work it out, the more you will be drained; the more frustrated, anxious, despairing, depressed, and unhinged you will

feel. **Manipulative individuals don't suddenly become genuine – you have to give up that fantasy.** What inevitably happens is that the psychopath will then employ a variety of increasingly convoluted tools and tactics to confuse you and get their way.

They will create drama, lie, blame you, make you feel guilty or talk in circles. They may make grand promises and apologies that won't be kept. **It's a losing battle.** Fighting losing battles **will only weaken your own energy and confidence reserves.** Continued exertion of energy to make them change will only lead to wasted time, increased frustration, and feelings of powerlessness, hopelessness, and eventual depression on your part.

2. They may view your independent action and assertion of your needs as an instance of their 'losing' or losing control, which will invite revenge and punishment at a later time.

3. If you reveal your true feelings and how you are hurt, you are exposing your weaknesses. Psychopaths are inherent predators who will exploit any weakness. Instead of changing behaviors like a normal person might, they will push your buttons further and prey on your weaknesses to sadistically hurt, manipulate, or control you.

The only permanent solution in dealing with a ruthless social exploiter is refusing all social interactions with them whatsoever.

Chapter 4
The Female Psychopath

"You can fool all the people some of the time, and some of the people all the time, but you cannot fool all the people all the time."

– Abraham Lincoln

Please bear in mind that this chapter is about female psychopaths and their traits and by no means refers to all women. As with previous chapters, possessing one or two of these traits does not guarantee that somebody is a psychopath. This chapter is predominately written for the male audience and contains some general statements on men and women that may cause offense if you take them as applying to everyone. These statements are there to serve a purpose – helping the intended audience to identify and avoid female predators.

Why is the Female Psychopath Hard to Spot?

Psychopathy is a gender-neutral phenomenon. Yet the female types are harder to spot due to better camouflage in society. Using a metaphor, looking at the female psychopath is like looking at the same traits as the male, but through two cloudy lenses. Or we can call them two smokescreens.

The best way to show this is in the diagram below.

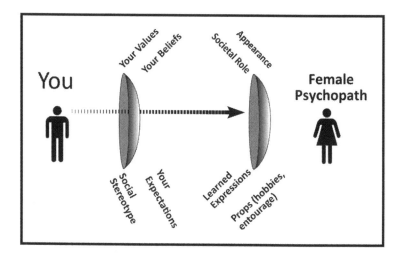

The first lens, or smokescreen, is your own. These are your expectations of females and the associations you attach to women. They are your ideals and projections, typically shaped by social influence and personal experience.

The second smokescreen is the persona the female psychopath creates. This facade exists on the outer surface of a person, separate from what is inside.

This can be made up of:

- Physical appearance, and the accouterments that create an image and impression (makeup, hair, clothing).

- The role assumed in society (nurse, caretaker, lawyer, expert).

- Learned body language and mimic behaviors (appearance of sensitivity, compassion, remorse, friendly smiles, good eye contact).

- Props (degrees, titles, entourage of admirers).

- Actions designed for a purpose (charity volunteer, churchgoer, dog lover).

- How much others have bought into their carefully calculated image (popularity, reputation, others' opinions).

Metaphorically speaking, the females are harder to detect because you are working with two sets of smokescreens, not just one.

All psychopaths, male or female, are adept at creating personas to fool people (one smokescreen). But the difference between the male and female versions is the traditional views and expectations of the feminine that still exist with many people – this can create an additional layer of clouded bias that prevents you from seeing them clearly (another smokescreen).

When you encounter a female psychopath, your judgment and viewpoint can then be filtered through two layers of extra 'stuff' that might make it *that much harder* to see who they truly are.

Now, do you see why it might be harder to spot a female psychopath?

For example, let's imagine the following situation:

A teary-eyed mother is advocating for her child. She wears a matronly sweater with a long flowery skirt. Her hair is shoulder length, a little frizzy. She has a protective and caring expression on her face. She's holding a baby and a four-year-old protectively, and she's saying the right words. Her goal? To portray an image of a loving, caring and vulnerable mother to secure resources (housing and money) from the state, or from her ex-husband, all in the name of her children.

What can possibly be so threatening about a mother begging for resources to care for her innocent children? Wouldn't that scenario tug at your heartstrings? Never in one hundred years would most people suspect hidden abuse or deceit. She may physically batter her children, burn them, or may even kill them.

Behind closed doors, this is what happens.

Society expects women to be nurturing. We have the image of a maternal ideal imprinted in our minds. For the psychopath, though, it's a role and an act. All psychopaths use and exploit their children. The hidden agenda is usually money.

How Do You Recognize a Female Psychopath? What are the Key Red Flags?

In Chapter 1, we have already compiled a thorough list of characteristics to help you identify a psychopath, which applies to both male and female versions.

Since men are the primary targets of female predators, in this section we have compiled a supplemental list and guide to help men identify a female psychopath quickly. Although focused on romantic contexts, it can also be useful in friendship and other scenarios.

Before we move on to the list, one of the most important things to keep in mind in a relationship with a psychopath is the critical component of *time*. Typically, the more time you spend in the relationship, the more severe the eventual harm and loss, and the harder it is to get out. Hence, to help the reader, we've organized the red flags by time, or the progression of your relationship, covering those red flags you will see immediately at the beginning of your romance, and those that gradually reveal themselves.

Our goal in highlighting these red flags is prevention by identifying them in the early stages of your relationship so that you can leave before further damage or entrapment occurs.

Time is critical for the following reasons:

1. Most people are blinded by the spark of initial chemistry. What they don't realize is that initial chemistry has nothing to do with things that sustain a healthy relationship – the compatibility of values, morals, outlooks, and life di-

rection. You can hit it off with someone right off the bat, and you can just as easily have chemistry with someone with a severe character disorder (a thief, murderer, criminal), as you can with a sane and healthy person. But the problem is, almost everyone is on their best behavior at first. Initial chemistry causes your guard to drop. By the time you have solid evidence that something is 'off', much time has been invested and wasted.

Furthermore, your infatuation and emotions now bind you, often resulting in emotional conflict. This makes it harder to act rationally in the best interest of your well-being.

2. All psychopaths try to brainwash and control you with manipulation, lies, and self-esteem killing tactics. Their methods often operate unconsciously and creep up on you unawares. However, the more *time* progresses with your subconscious boundaries eliminated, the more dependent you become. There's a real danger you may gradually become too weak to make the firm resolution to break free.

3. The more time passes, the more you invest emotionally, socially, physically, and financially. A relationship with a female psychopath *never* ends well, so the bigger your expectations, investment, and elation, the harder your fall. Financial loss, heartbreak and emotional hurt are compounded. If you catch the warning signs early, it is possible to minimize the damage on all fronts.

4. Last but not least, leaving in the early stages can save your life. Psychopaths are power addicts. They derive sadistic enjoyment from inflicting pain. Because this personality type needs a constant supply of power at anoth-

er's expense, they need to constantly up the ante for the same effect. Very much like a drug addict developing a tolerance to a drug, they need a larger dose to achieve the same response as before. This means once you give an inch, their mistreatment and abuse always escalates over time and never diminishes. If you stay long enough, it eventually culminates in physical violence and threats.

Imagine being abused when you fall sick, weak, or have a life-threatening illness. She won't be there to support you. Instead, she will abuse you when you are helpless and help push you over the edge. Female psychopaths will also incite you to violence, so they can call the police and press false charges. All it takes is one such incident to permanently damage your record and your life.

The Six Red Flags in the Love Bombing Stage

This first list outlines six red flags *all* female psychopaths have in common during the love bombing stage. Just as with any psychopath, a female psychopath is on her best behavior in the early days and the target will only experience the charming, surface persona.

Each of the six traits and behaviors serves a purpose. They elicit subconscious reactions in a target. For easier reference, the six traits and behaviors are summarized in the following chart, then expanded later.

Again, *all* female psychopaths display the big six when they are trying to hook you. Individually, one or two red flags do not mean she is a psychopath. But, the more red flags she displays, the more your suspicion should be heightened to possible character flaws. If she exhibits all six, this is a profile of a predator.

The Six Red Flags in the Love Bombing Stage

	What Is It?	What Does It Do?
1. High Testosterone	Key psychopathic trait	Hooks and attracts you
2. Professional Victim	Manipulative tactic	Lowers your defenses Wins your trust
3. Rushes into the Relationship and Sex	Manipulative tactic	Lowers your defenses Induces dependence
4. Excessive Flattery	Manipulative tactic	Lowers your defenses Wins your trust Induces dependence
5. Beautiful Promises	Manipulative tactic	Lowers your defenses Wins your trust Induces dependence
6. Strange and Unlikely Tales	Key psychopathic trait	Prerequisite to possible pathological liar

1. High testosterone

All psychopaths possess high levels of the hormone testosterone. The female ones may not be as overtly bombastic as the male version since certain illusions of 'femininity' can be achieved with makeup, hair, dress, and other props. However, this hormone always manifests itself in a consistent and telling pattern of traits and behaviors:

- Very charismatic with strong sexual magnetism
- High sex drive
- Aggressive behavior
- Power hungry, desiring to hold power over men
- Upper body strength
- Possible Adam's apple.[1]

2. Professional victim

A female psychopath will always have stories of victimization. Stories about an abusive father, mother, extended family, or ex-boyfriends. They may claim to have been abused physically, emotionally, and/or sexually. These stories are often told in a contrived climate of intimacy. Playing the victim needs to be established during the love bombing stage because:

a) It elicits pity in the target, who may feel sorry for them and treat them with special care.

b) It allows a target's mind to make excuses for strange, abnormal behavior. You end up tolerating much more abuse than you would have otherwise.

c) It lowers a target's guard substantially, as they falsely believe the female psychopath is a harmless, vulnerable victim who needs help.

Grounded reality: Think about it. Abuse is a very sensitive topic. Those who are truly abused are unlikely to go around sharing it with those they just met. You may not know about it until you are close friends for years, sometimes decades. Typically, real victims value privacy, others' perception of them, and don't wish to relive the pain. Individuals who are positive and self-reliant also want to come across as strong, non-tarnished, and would never want to be seen as a victim. If someone you just met shares highly personal details that elicit pity, this is a red flag to ask yourself why? What are their motives for doing so?

3. Rushes into the relationship and sex

Psychopaths always click immediately with you and seem to have a lot in common with you.

Knowing men are susceptible to sex, she will use it to lure you in. She is seductive, has sex with you soon after you meet, and says I love you within a span of weeks. She will claim a soulmate connection and that she never felt this way about anyone else before in her life. There will be intense sex sessions, and the relationship advances at a dazzling speed. You feel euphoric, delirious, hypnotized, as if in a spell. Targets always say it felt too good to be true.

Alternatively, if she has read self-help books saying that men prefer to wait for sex, a sly psychopath may intentionally delay sex to win your trust. This depends on her agenda, but she will flaunt her sexuality in obvious ways and dangle it to keep you hooked.

Grounded reality: Solid relationships in real life are built slowly, on secure foundations, not dreams, soulmates, and illusions. Whereas predators want you dazed and confused, they want you to loosen your guard, so you are easily exploited and controlled. Here are two questions to ask yourself:

a) If she has sex with you so rapidly, what may that imply about her values?

b) Genuine 'soulmate' type connections do happen, of course but rarely. In the event she is not a predator and truly feels such strong emotions, but chooses to rush the relationship without thinking, what does that say about her decision-making/life skills? Why isn't she more cautious and self-protective?

4. Excessive flattery

Flattery is a key tool in *every psychopath's* arsenal. It is designed to release high levels of the mood-elevating chemical dopamine. Targets quickly become emotionally dependent, the end result being an altered person who is highly susceptible to suggestion. Men are especially susceptible to female flattery because it massages the male ego. Her sweet talk is over the top, sycophantic, or continuous. For example, initially, everything about you is amazing. You are the best lover, most capable, most talented man she's ever met! The most vulnerable targets are those who need female approval to feel good about themselves.

Grounded reality: Learn to always suspect the motives behind flattery and stay grounded. Genuine people make compliments occasionally, but they are not excessive. Over the top flattery is designed to manipulate the target for personal and financial gain. Many people use flattery to advance themselves in life, and they are not necessarily psychopathic. However, the more excessive the flattery, especially combined with other red flags, the more dangerous her motive.

5. Beautiful promises

A female psychopath always promises eternal love and devotion. *Every single one does this.* They will plant notions in your subconscious mind that they are in it for the long haul, and give you visions of an amazing future. The promises can be anything – usually whatever angle they sense may work you best. For example, declarations to the tune of *"I will never leave you," "I will never hurt you," "I will take care of you when you get old,"* are common.

Grounded reality: First, remember, words mean nothing. It is actions built up over time that mean anything of substance. People who make fast or excessive promises are to be suspected, not trusted. Second, who can possibly predict the future? A promise means a great deal to a person of real conscience and character; they will *never* make a promise so easily or quickly.

6. Strange and unlikely tales

Psychopaths are pathological liars who cannot distinguish between truth and lies. This is hard to detect at first. During the initial meetings with a female psychopath, a man cannot possibly know the information fed to them is lies. However, how this particular trait *will manifest* are strings of stories about their past and their backgrounds that seem unbelievable, doubtful, outrageous, cannot be substantiated, or facts that just don't add up.

Grounded reality: A target male needs to trust their instincts. Once there is evidence of lies, trust is broken. It's up to you to apply ruthless logic and take appropriate action. If someone can look you in the eyes so convincingly and lie to you, what else can they be lying about? How can you be friends with someone you don't trust?

If you learn to recognize the big six, a female predator can hold no power over you. No matter how subtle the execution, you will recognize the traits for what they are, and what they do to a target subconsciously. Then evade and extract yourself in time.

The Secondary Red Flags

As you get to know her better, more traits are revealed. The red flags in this category usually appear when a relationship is semi-established.

Remember, most psychopaths escape notice until intimate, personal encounters. This is where the real person seeps out from the initial facade. The timing can be weeks, months, or years. How fast her true self reveals itself will fluctuate, based on individual circumstances, powers of observation and interactions.

Sexual red flags

- Eventually, you will find out she's extremely promiscuous. She has sexual relations with a wide variety of people behind your back, often for money or other gains with a prostitute mentality.

- She may request violent or deviant sex. There may be unexpected sexual arousal, seeming to get off from violence, pain, sadism, and debasement.

- She may have affairs with both men and women. Psychopaths lack a firm gender identity. What's important to them is the intoxication of power from conquering other human beings, regardless of the target's gender. Hence, a psychopath may use the term 'bisexual' or 'lesbian' and such nomenclatures that give her a socially accepted identity, but this is not the underlying root cause.

Behavioral red flags

- She begins to exhibit violent rages, psychotic outbursts, and impulsive and irrational behavior. If you are not married yet, the behavior will be intermittent – she will be hot and cold. The frequency, length, and intensity of abuse escalate in direct proportion to how much she feels you are in her clutches.

- Slowly, you notice she feels no remorse or guilt for wrongdoing and cannot produce real empathy. For example, she reacts to death and traumatic events in abnormal ways. There may be staged words or actions, but it won't feel real or sincere. You notice she enjoys inflicting pain and seeing you tortured. Psychopaths tend to enjoy the pain of others; it makes them feel powerful and alive.

- She complains that you are crazy or need psychological help, particularly when you start questioning her. This is a common pattern, as most psychopaths project their disorder on to those intimate with them.

- She expects you to pay for everything but does not reciprocate, giving various excuses. Besides sex, you notice she never does anything for you that is personally meaningful or genuinely in your best interest – it's all self-serving and the give and take is grossly unequal. Remember, psychopaths form relationships for supply and a meal ticket. *You* are the meal ticket.

Social red flags

- The first thing you notice will be unreasonable jealousy. She's jealous of the attention you give to your friends, family and even children. She's obsessively jealous of other females, often reacting irrationally to small, innocent things, such as a compliment or a look. This behavior is not rooted in any type of normal insecurity, but a psychological disorder. The more unreasonable the jealousy, the more serious the psychosis.

- You notice she has few real friends, if any. Her female friendships are more likely to be with less attractive, plain, overweight, or ugly women. This is a pattern with female psychopaths, wanting to hoard all the attention and to look more attractive in her friends' company.

- You notice a sharp dichotomy in how she treats people. She's haughty and demeaning towards service people and others with no perceived value but turns to instant charm the moment someone 'important' arrives on the scene. Her behavior conflicts with her stated values (words), and don't match up with her public image.

What are Female Psychopaths' Tools? How Do They Behave Differently to the Male?

Female and male psychopaths have similar motivations. As natural parasites and predators, both want control, money, and power. The main difference is their means.

All psychopaths exploit societal norms to achieve their ends. Those social conventions are nothing but a prop, tool, and method to conveniently use and masquerade under, in order to get what they are really after. Being the female gender simply means their base instincts are better disguised in society. In other words, on a cursory glance, the behaviors of a female psychopath fit closer to societal norms and people's social expectations.

But let's take the blinders off.

The following tables provide a quick snapshot of the psychopath's main tools. They translate and summarize each stereotypical, social convention to how the female psychopath will exploit and manipulate it, *as a means to an end.*

The Main Lure

The tool: *Sex*

How it's used and manipulated: Men's desire for sex is a female psychopath's most powerful weapon. Sex does not affect a psychopath, as there is no emotional attachment. Female psychopaths will deploy this primary tool promiscuously.

The tool: *Attractive Appearance*

How it's used and manipulated: In our society, a woman is often judged based on her looks. This is a big advantage for the female psychopath. All she needs to do is invest time in a beautiful, feminine masquerade, and no one will notice her disorder.

The tool: *Love*

How it's used and manipulated: Love is the primary construct a female psychopath uses to ensnare unsuspecting men, usually to underwrite their expensive lifestyles. Men are susceptible to female attention. Female psychopaths can't feel love, but they can imitate it very well.

The tool: *Relationships*

How it's used and manipulated: For a social predator, relationships are the singular route for exploitation. Female psychopaths, like the male, view people as energy sources and objects to use and discard. They form relationships to ruthlessly exploit and destroy, but under the guise of 'care', 'love', and 'friendship'.

Social Concepts

The tool: *The Helpless, Weaker Sex*

How it's used and manipulated: This social norm is a big advantage for the female psychopath. Society views women as the weaker sex, evoking the protector/provider instinct in the male. The female psychopath will exploit this by playing the role of a sensitive being and a perpetual victim. The 'damsel in distress' facade hides her cold, cunning, and callous nature. Inducing sympathy also gains her attention while lowering the man's defenses against her machinations.

The tool: *The Trophy Girlfriend/Wife*

How it's used and manipulated: Two prevalent social concepts are at work here: beautiful women are viewed as luxury commodities and they marry into money. A female psychopath will exploit those social constructs by positioning herself as the trophy girlfriend in the dating marketplace, eliciting men to lavish money on her for her sexual favors. The difference between her and someone genuine boils down to her agenda, which is solely material, and exploitation focused. There are no true feelings of partnership, caring, or fidelity. Most male victims won't realize this until it's too late.

Relationship Tools

The tool: *Pregnancy*

How it's used and manipulated: Pregnancy will not be a natural occurrence, but rather a means to an end. If she needs temporary shelter, she may fake pregnancy. If a man seems like a good, long-term meal ticket, she will become pregnant to manipulate him into marriage, or to acquire child support payments.

The tool: *Marriage*

How it's used and manipulated: To a psychopath, marriage is simply a construct used to entrap a prey, so she won't have to work. The real goals are legally sanctioned financial exploitation and abuse. Underneath that piece of paper, there will be no love, fidelity, friendship, or caring. The only difference here between the behavior of a male and a female psychopath is that the female stay-at-home partner is more socially accepted and sanctioned.

The tool: *Motherhood*

How it's used and manipulated: Motherhood is simply a construct that allows her to play the role of a nurturer and caretaker in return for gains, monetarily or in social acceptance. A female psychopath cannot connect with her children. She can't love, and she possesses no empathy. Beneath a maternal image and behind closed doors, there is often abuse and exploitation.

The tool: *Children*

How it's used and manipulated: The female psychopath does not care about her children's well-being – they are tools and possessions to be exploited. In accordance with her value system, her children are often prostituted, literally or figuratively. There will be a distinct public/private behavior. Abuse is often hidden under respectable personas. In marriages and court battles, children are used as hostages in personal vendettas against the father, or to guarantee maintenance payments.

Emotional Manipulation Tools

The tool: *Flattery*

How it's used and manipulated: Gushing flattery is a key manipulation tool. Many men need and depend on female praise to feel worthy, which makes them highly susceptible targets. Used in the love bombing stage, flattery causes the brain to release the feel-good chemical dopamine. A target can easily become dependent on this chemical high and gradually place their self-esteem in the hands of the psychopath.

The tool: *Hysterics*

How it's used and manipulated: Female psychopaths are often violent, prone to rages and hysterical outbursts. Because society believes women are more 'emotional', it can easily be mistaken as stereotypical female drama. In reality, this is a weapon used for control.

The tool: *Tears*

How it's used and manipulated: All psychopaths use 'crocodile tears' to induce pity. As society assigns vulnerability and depth of feeling to the feminine, tears can be even more powerful when used by a female psychopath. Those tears attract 'white knights' who want to protect the female, and who feel guilt hurting someone who's seemingly weaker. But her emotions are always faked, never real.

The tool: *Jealousy*

How it's used and manipulated: Female psychopaths are irrationally and hatefully jealous. This trait is easily disguised or viewed as stereotypical female insecurity. Their jealousy, however, is rooted in a mental disorder, not normal pettiness.

The tool: *Submissiveness*

How it's used and manipulated: At the love bombing stage, a female psychopath will feign submissiveness and self-abasement. When used in combination with flattery, it props up the male ego. However, this 'submissiveness' isn't real; it's just a manipulation tool. Her true nature will unfold in time.

The tool: *Cooking*

How it's used and manipulated: Most people develop cooking skills from genuine interest. A female psychopath learns to cook to manipulate. Home-cooked meals are connected to primal feelings of nurture, comfort, and nourishment. People tend to trust those that feed them. Thus, psychopaths often prepare single meals or elaborate parties to manipulate their image or their target's emotions.

Other Tools

The tool: *Aggression*

How it's used and manipulated: While male psychopaths display aggression through overt violence, the female psychopath tends to rely on covert aggression. She is equally vicious, but uses psychological and emotional tactics to hurt, dominate, intimidate, and humiliate.

The tool: *Method of Bullying*

How it's used and manipulated: Unlike the male, female psychopaths usually bully in packs. They use cliques and social isolation as instruments of destruction. There is always a leader that incites drama, poisons relationships, and pits people against each other. The goal is usually to outcast a female target.

The tool: *Work and Career*

How it's used and manipulated: While many careers are possible, female psychopaths often hide themselves in caring professions such as nursing and social work. If she does not wish to work, she will use the euphemism of 'giving up her career for family or children' as a nice sounding front.

The tool: *Feminism*

How it's used and manipulated: She may claim she is a feminist when convenient. In reality, she views all other females as threats – one-upmanship is the goal. Like everything else, feminism is nothing more than a construct she may use to acquire power, popularity, supporters, and other benefits.

Why are Men Easy Targets for the Female Psychopath? Why is the Female Psychopath More Dangerous than the Male?

A relationship with a female psychopath is akin to a man in a tank with a shark – one that wears the mask of feminine daintiness but plays a ruthless game under a disguise of love.

In our society, the reality is that men are often easier targets who suffer worse consequences. This is due to the following reasons:

1. You don't see them coming. Many men take the feminine at face value rather than understanding the whole person, or hidden motives behind surface gestures. You just don't expect to see cruel, deceitful, cunning behaviors in women.

2. Many men cannot resist a sexual enticement. Female psychopaths are often sexually magnetic. They may use sex as a lure, and later on a tool for power and control. It is easy to get ensnared. For example, if a female psychopath has an affair with a married man, she may use this to blackmail him throughout the relationship and when it ends.

3. Many men are ego driven. The female psychopath has many weapons to play on the male ego, such as flattery, lavishing attention, and playing the victim. Her carefully constructed image can be beautiful and popular, positioning herself as a 'trophy' to be won. Since many guys only want what other guys want, they become so dis-

tracted by the chase and the ego-boost she gives them that it blinds them to important red flags.

4. Female psychopaths typically target conscientious men, who are taught to be gallant to all women and never physically attack or harm them. She, on the other hand, has no such scruples. This unequal playing field gives the female abuser a huge advantage.

5. When a man does fight back or refuses to cooperate, a common tactic for the female psychopath is to fake abuse claims. As soon as the word 'abuse' is uttered, protective forces in society can be biased towards the alleged female victim. The target male can find himself in all sorts of trouble, with police, the court system, and social workers involved. He may be threatened with jail and a domestic abuse record, even if he is innocent and the one being abused. Those tactics make otherwise sane and reasonable men feel powerless.

6. Once the female psychopath has exploited, abused, or discarded her target, the man often feels ashamed. Compared with female victims, he has fewer support groups to help manage the after effects and the severe psychological damage. Lastly, by societal standards, it's less acceptable for a man to be 'abused' by a woman. Fearing ridicule and stigma, many men end up suffering in silence, prolonging the pain.

What Type of Men Do the Female Psychopaths Target?

In general, the female psychopath is attracted to those that offer money, excitement (promise of thrills), or simply an opportunity for an easy meal ticket.

The following men are the most susceptible:

1. Men who are naive, trusting to a fault, or inexperienced in the dating world. Men who may not recognize the red flags at the beginning of the relationship, what they portend down the road, and who don't act on them until it's too late.

2. Men who want to be the rescuer, a white knight to a helpless female. (This mentality has nothing to do with age.) The female psychopath plays the victim role very well. Pity mongering is a key tactic.

3. Men who are just out of a divorce, breakup, or other traumatic life event. They are in a transitional, recovery, and rebound phase, with their defenses at the weakest. A female vulture is adept at detecting vulnerability and prefers easy targets.

4. In general, people who look for love and strength externally, outside of themselves. To a predator, your void and neediness is an opportunity. A smart psychopath can quickly construct the persona of your dream woman for her own devious ends.

How Does a Romantic Relationship with a Female Psychopath End?

No matter how well the relationship begins, it generally ends badly for the target.

The female psychopath will drain the target physically, emotionally, financially, and socially (through isolation and slander).

The chart on the following page explains it best – with the best-case scenario, worst-case scenario, and a wide middle spectrum of possibilities.

Please note the chart enables a big picture understanding. It does not necessarily encompass all situations that a disordered person can wreck in your life.

Best-case scenario – If you are lucky, it usually ends with a petty exploitation of some sort, along with a smear campaign of various intensity launched behind your back.

Middle scenario – In the chart, the middle spectrum lists five of the most common outcomes. Between the best and the worst case, a wide range of deceitful and destructive behaviors are possible.

Worst-case scenario – The absolute worst case needs to be taken seriously. Premeditated murder occurs behind closed doors in shrouds of secrecy, most often with financial incentives.

How does it typically end?

Best-case Scenario:	• Cold, callous, sudden discard.	**All scenarios include the following:**
	• Petty theft of money or possessions.	
	• Smear campaign to your social and work network.	• Social isolation
	• Blackmail and threats. Often to gain money and possessions.	• Psychological damage
	• Claim to be pregnant by you. Her motives are control, free food, accommodation, or child support.	• Damaged sense of self
Middle Scenario:	• Identity theft and forged signature of financial documents. Potential bankruptcy and financial ruin for you.	• Damaged self-esteem
		• Depression, stress, anxiety
	• Falsely accuse you of assault, rape, abuse. May result in jail time and a criminal record.	• May take years to recover
	• If married with children, she will take your house, alimony and child support. You are the long-term meal ticket.	
	• Drives you to suicide.	
	• Murder to collect life insurance and/or inheritance money.	
Worst-case Scenario:	• Falsification of your Will.	

How Do Female Psychopaths Treat Other Females?

The female psychopath will see everything in terms of competition and female aggression. They view all other females as threats, and they can never be objective.

When an empathetic female encounters a female psychopath at work, home or social venues, the empath, naturally fair-minded and considerate to others, is often completely bewildered and confused at the veiled attacks, hatred and damage that ensues. However, the psychopath's behaviors are predictable. The best way to understand these behaviors is to view everything comprehensively using the analogy of the interconnected cycle of the combustion engine, relating to:

- Their motivation
- The targets
- Their tactics

Motivation – this means how they are wired inside, how the engine works, the internal mechanism that drives all outward behaviors.

Targets – the gasoline, and the external spark that accidentally sets off the faulty wiring. This is not the target's fault. Most targets are unaware that their natural qualities are setting off another's warped issues. Since female psychopaths often engage in a one-sided competition, most targets do not even know they are targets until it's too late.

Tactics – outward behaviors. This is a predictable outcome of combining the engine (how things are wired) and gasoline (what triggers it), causing direct ignition.

Without understanding how the internal mechanism works and the complete cycle, one can only grasp surface behaviors at a very superficial level.

What is the Female Psychopath's General Motivation?

Her ultimate motivation is to destroy beauty, love, conscience, and femininity, rooted out of instinctive loathing and jealousy. This destruction mechanism exists at a deep, subconscious level. Self-awareness differs within the individual but the results (the ignition) are the same nonetheless.

The best way to understand it is via masculine and feminine archetypes. Everyone possesses masculine and feminine energy inside of them. Masculine energy is associated with action, assertiveness, sex drive, how they fight, how they express anger, and how they go about achieving goals. Feminine energy is associated with empathy, love, caring, beauty, and what they value. Most individuals are balanced or tilted towards one particular side, and it defines their day-to-day personality.

With female psychopaths, not only do they have a weak feminine side, its expression is twisted and distorted. She views all feminine qualities (empathy, love, and caring) as weaknesses. Despising those qualities deep inside, she is incapable of treating females who symbolize and exhibit those qualities in a healthy manner.

At the same time, there is also instinctive jealousy. She is aware that other females have something that she does not. While she can emulate the superficial components of femininity, be it via looks, behavior, dress, etc., no amount of surface artifice can possibly replicate what is true and real – because she cannot possess the qualities she covets, she's bent on destroying them in others.

Who Do They Target?

Female psychopaths will target people who have something they envy but cannot have; usually those that possess beauty, intelligence, who radiate femininity, warmth, love, moral character, etc.

For example, in the work environment, they will target classy, highly educated females with a commendable work history. The female targets are usually responsible, capable, and highly qualified in their field of expertise. The psychopath will do everything in her power to undermine them and try to get them fired. Instead of seeking to help female subordinates advance, the female psychopath boss will feel threatened, especially if the underlings are younger, prettier, and intelligent.

What Are Their Tactics?

Both male and female psychopaths share the same motivations, but female aggression is usually more indirect.

The attacks are covert and can creep upon you unawares. Female aggression is cloaked in seemingly innocent behavior, or behavior so subtle you can't put your finger on it. The results can be more damaging because you don't see it coming. However, there is always a pattern. Below are the main tactics, which are used in combination or in different stages in time:

1. **Isolation and bullying** – Female psychopaths bully in packs. She uses female cliques as an instrument to exclude, isolate, and create situations where you alone face

a group. To do this, she often befriends 'lesser' females, manipulates their insecurities, and incites them to become her enablers and accomplices.

2. **Female gossip** – She will slander and drop malicious rumors through the grapevine or stir poison between relationships. This is a covert instrument to undermine, humiliate and demean. It allows her to hide while she destroys the target's good name, turns people against you, and wreaks havoc on your psyche. If confronted, she will deny it.

3. **Fake friend and sabotage** – She will pretend to be your friend to get to know all about you, then secretly backstabs. They are the masters of secret sabotage. Behind the smiles, she's an invisible enemy who's secretly engaged in a one-sided competition to tear you down.

4. **Emotional and psychological harassment** – In whatever way possible, she subjects her target to continual stress and harassment, and derives enjoyment from doing so.

Once you understand how this interconnected system works together, the behaviors are highly predictable.

In the real world, if you become a target of the female psychopath, you realize their behavior has nothing to do with you. Your niceness won't matter. Being extra kind won't help. Showing vulnerability will not soften them. Befriending them won't work. It's simply what you 'represent' and who they are.

People who are in tune with their feminine energy (those who are loving, caring and possess empathy) will naturally appreciate, enjoy, and even cherish the same quality in others, not seek to destroy or sabotage.

Chapter 5
Understanding Them
More Deeply

"Three things cannot be long hidden: the sun, the moon, and the truth."

– Buddha

This section was compiled for those who require deeper insights and are unsatisfied with psychopathy as it is presented – as a modern-day clinical condition. Thus, it may not be applicable or useful to everyone. When personal experience of the psychopath hits us, the full impact of the existence of these people often brings up many more unanswered questions within belief systems.

What is the Spiritual Purpose of a Psychopath? Why Do These People Exist on This Planet?

According to certain spiritual schools of thought, everyone is born with certain lessons they must learn in this lifetime. People come into our lives to teach us the necessary lessons we need to learn at the right times. Everything in the universe exists for a reason.

For the targets, the ultimate purpose is to shed every part of yourself to the very core through pain and purification, to reach your truest essence. An encounter with a psychopath comes as the universe's unwitting teacher, forced into a state of crisis. With pain often comes transformation and necessary growth. This is a spiritual lesson to see the world as it truly is, not a manufactured preconception of socially acceptable standards. It's good to see yourself as you truly are, purified from artifice. Those who are inherently positive and strong survive, thrive, and learn.

Everyone's lessons are different. Most often, the individual will undergo a deep shift in their value systems, which previously may have adapted to the prevailing social standards of conformist behavior – the pursuit of material pleasure and superficial illusory goods. Now, by plunging deep to examine their own motivations and beliefs and to eliminate the false, they become aware of a deeper reality. The search for truth often produces a stronger character, formed upon inner values that are true, real, and permanent. Once transformed, they move forward to a better purpose. The lessons are frequently not apparent until years later.

For the psychopath themselves, the ultimate purpose is through eventual loss and the complete shedding and destruction of everything they considered valuable and stubbornly held on to. They learn to abandon any deep-seated conception that they can own, control, or possess something tangible on the earthly plane, and they eventually probe deep within for intangible spiritual fulfillment. In short, their value and relating system requires a painful overhaul. If this spiritual lesson is not learned in this lifetime, they will be reborn again with the same issues to resolve.

We can now explore how this eventual destruction takes place. Purely psychopathic individuals are born with an intrinsic belief system of a **lack of abundance**, which is why they must take, defraud, control, and rape from others what they can get, typically through manipulation, force, and other questionable tactics. What they are blind to are the unseen laws of nature. Those tactics and lack of conscience eventually lead to ruin, loss, and destruction of the things they originally valued in the first place – money, power, sex, position, and so on.

Is it self-fulfilling prophecy or destiny? That's hard to say.

Why Does the Psychopath Blame the Partner So Much in a Relationship? Why Can't They Ever Be Happy?

This is really *their* problem, not their partner's.

Here is how this mechanism works:

1. Firstly, they think of a partner as a **situation** or **object**. Unable to view or relate to them as a human being with needs and feelings that need to be continuously reciprocated, they simply want to get the most out of this object or situation.

2. They imagine that love takes them to extreme passion and spiritual heights, partially because society glorifies these unrealistic expectations and partially as an internal belief.

3. However, they never experience the extreme passion or spiritual height they imagined. So, they blame their partner for not creating or providing the 'situation' in which they can feel this high.

4. Unable to relate to people with affection and empathy, what they do feel in relationships are the thrills of winning. **To them, this may be experienced as 'love' or 'passion'.** This is their concept of love, and the only emotion they are capable of feeling at their level of development.

5. But they will need more and more input to continue to feel that thrill. Each new boundary violation and new low the partner experiences in submission and subjugation, the psychopath wins in domination, gaining a temporary thrill. However, the psychopath's need for emo-

tional nourishment is a black hole that can never be satisfied.

6. No human being on earth is capable of continuously giving themselves up with their own needs unmet, without causing destruction to themselves. It's a matter of time before they leave or get destroyed or discarded because their energies have been used up.

7. The pattern repeats with a new target.

Bottom line:

The real problem is their own nature, their inability to love and relate. Without an awareness to probe internally, they're a lost cause. True happiness in love requires equal give and take of emotional nourishment. If all their past relationships fit the same warped pattern and yours don't follow the same patterns, the only common denominator is them.

Are All Psychopaths the Same? Why Do Some Behave in Prescribed Patterns and Not Others?

A frequent question one encounters is: why do some psychopaths seem capable of empathy and care? Conventional explanations state that everything is a mask hiding the real person underneath. While in the majority of the cases the 'mask explanation' is accurate, reality often holds more dimension and nuance than the simplified explanation.

Not all psychopaths are the same. There are three factors that may explain different experiences with and between psychopathic personalities.

1. There are limits to using modern psychiatry to understand nature.

First, psychopathy and sociopathy are basically modern terminologies. Yet this type of person has existed throughout history; longer than modern science has been in existence. Some believe that the age-old folklore of vampires – the draining of life energy, a continuous stream of victims, the inability to be satiated – are symbolisms inspired from this **personality archetype**.

It's only recently we have put a scientific label on the psychopathy phenomenon. One thing to remember is that psychology and psychiatry are still, relatively speaking, in their infancy. There is still much we don't know about how the brain works. Every couple of years, the Diagnostic and Statistical Manual (DSM) changes its rules for various disorders and diseases, as new studies find results that refute old results. The field has often been called an inexact science.

The research and structure of the manual are useful guides, but it's also wise to keep an open mind. The field itself is fluid and ever-changing. Current research may not offer a comprehensive view to understanding nature.

2. Don't confuse personal *values* with personality *expression*.

Personal values are a deeply held, ingrained, character-based belief system. This system affects empathy, world views, morals and ethics, and caring about others' welfare versus exploiting them. Values are implicitly related to choice; they guide decisions by allowing for an individual's choices to reflect their moral beliefs or non-beliefs.

Personality expressions are, in some sense, more superficial. They are preferences in taste: likes, dislikes, and different manners of expressing individual energies. For example, being funny or solemn, liking the color blue or yellow, gravitating toward parties and the center of attention versus a preference for small groups, or a sweet, sensitive, sympathetic mannerism – these are all personality expressions.

If someone's personality expression matches what you are naturally attracted to, it is possible to have warm feelings for them, even fall in love with them. But remember, ultimately *values and character* are what determine how someone treats you in their actions and decisions.

Psychopathy is a mental disorder rooted in the **personal value system**, not in **personality expression**. There is a dysfunction with the way the psychopath relates to other human beings that proves dangerous for those involved.

All psychopaths have similarities in value systems, but differences in personality expression. For example, a psychopath's preference for a large family, family environment, or a 'family person' image is an expression. But how they treats their family members – perhaps lying, exploiting, cheating, and engaging in other abusive or criminal activities behind the scenes – are all driven by their internal value system.

When we differentiate between **personal values** and **personality expression**, we can then understand why individual psychopaths can express their tastes differently, yet certain external patterns driven by their internal value system are similar between psychopaths.

3. People are inherently complex, with varying components to their personalities.

Essentially, everyone's personalities are different, with different facets and components. We all have good sides and not-so-good sides.

- Our everyday actions and judgments depend on which forces inside of us are stronger.

- Many people have internal conflicts between different desires.

- What we ultimately put into action may depend on which side wins out.

- Other individuals can draw out certain facets and energies within us (as opposed to other characteristics, creating 'chemistry').

Personality components are a common human denominator. They apply to everyone.

Hence, some psychopaths may seem empathetic or kind, through certain sides of their personality. Some may have detached and intellectual sides to them, some violent and cruel. It may even be possible for some to have quite wonderful personality components.

However, the key difference to remember is that, with a psychopath, their *relating disorder* (lack of empathy, remorse, seeing people as objects) is one of the strongest forces in their character, driving and dominating the personality and overriding all other personality components.

It is a **potent, deep, primal instinct**, which, even if hidden by facades or not immediately visible, will eventually surface in intimate association.

The dependent factors are simply time and proximity – how long you know them and how closely you are involved with them.

How Do Psychopaths Interact with Each Other?

All psychopaths are exploitative takers who prey on and surround themselves with givers. It's against their nature to waste time on other takers. In most cases, there's no reason for them to engage.

However, psychopaths don't always recognize each other immediately. They all wear masks to hide their true intent and they exist at various levels of functioning. Thus, the mutual deception can go on for a while.

Based on my research, the dynamics between two psychopaths follow certain patterns. The psychopath who first recognizes the other is usually the one who's higher functioning, more intelligent, and more self-aware.

He or she eventually succeeds in a ploy to oust or discard the latter. The motive is either possession of competing resources or cutting losses. All psychopaths are possessive of their prey, position, and toys. In their eyes, there can only be one owner. Another predator is a threat that needs to be eliminated and a negative value that's a waste of energy.

In situations when there's mutual recognition between two psychopaths, they're usually at similar functioning and self-awareness levels. Three outcomes can typically arise:

1. They stay out of each other's way and hunt in their own territory. Unless there's a reason to cross paths, they are cognizant of the threat the other poses, and they prize self-preservation.

2. They work together temporarily on a common goal, whether it's a financial con, eliminating a common enemy, or a crime.

3. They can have an obsessive sexual relationship of limited duration, usually motivated by excitement and challenge.

When engagement occurs in outcomes 2 and 3 above, it's always due to utility and circumstance. There's no underlying trust, loyalty, or emotional bonds. Hence, if the circumstances or utility shifts, their relationship can change dramatically from disengagement to hatred and turning upon each other.

Chapter 6
How to Get Over Them
in Real Life

"Who looks outside, dreams; who looks inside, awakes."

– Carl Jung

Dealing with the Aftermath

After encounters with a psychopath, one of the most common problems empaths face is their (often accurate) perception of the injustice of how they were treated. We can examine ways to get over the ruin by looking at specific situations, like the following:

"I am recently separated and upset by the unfairness of the entire situation. My ex got the money, a new woman, and a happy life, and I am left with nothing. I am emotionally shattered and destroyed. How do I overcome this exceedingly unfair outcome?"

It may seem unbearably unfair on the surface but look deeper. Don't undersell the most valuable commodities that money just can't buy:

- Freedom
- Time
- Inner truth

Don't be jealous of the new partner. They are actually the victim. You are free to do anything now. You can rebuild, with a valuable lesson behind you. It can only get better from this point. At best, if the psychopath 'loves' the new partner in the only way they are capable of – they will be owned and controlled like a possession, with no freedom to direct their life. Over the long term, it's a psychological prison with dangerous consequences. At worst, the new target will be robbed of their money, trust, sanity, energy, and possibly health. They may be completely broken, a shadow of their former self. When he or she gets out, they are in for at least 12 months of deep recovery. **You now have everything open to you.**

Don't be jealous of him or her, or their life. Psychopaths never learn, and they never grow. They are trapped in a losing cycle dependent on the uncertain winds of fate.

Weak foundations – The psychopath has never developed the patience, work ethic, and character foundations that result in satisfying rewards. The sad thing is that they never will. Their motto will always be 'immediate gratification of the self' by deception and conning others.

Destroying their own futures – Just as they're incapable of considering anyone else's long-term interest, they're actually incapable of considering their own. Making enemies and spreading bitterness shoots themselves in the foot over the long term. They underestimate certain individuals' future capacity for influence, power, and success, or their willpower to get even.

Delusional thinking – Although most psychopaths feel no love and loyalty to anyone, they expect unconditional love and loyalty from those over whom they've established a dominance bond. Anything less is a justification for them to act out. This belief system is **delusional**. In real life, can such expectations ever result in interpersonal happiness? It's a hopeless, perpetual **lose-lose cycle**.

Outer image built upon sand – The only way the psychopath can continue their convincing presentation of success is by pulling increasingly bigger scams on unsuspecting targets. Always, underneath the presentation, they are hollow frauds. They can't control or change themselves internally for lasting fulfillment or success, and consequently, their illusory success depends on external factors that are outside of their own control. It's only a matter of time before things catch up with them – typically by offending the wrong powers, being involved in an incident that exposes their backgrounds, or mistaking an eagle for a lamb.

Can never feel the nourishment of love, truth, spiritual wisdom – Psychopaths are stuck with being a black hole, eternally empty. They need to constantly fill this hole with external things and temporary thrills. They will always live somewhat aimlessly, never experiencing a fulfilling life with purpose in their heart, or the soul-enriching quality of love and affection. And in most cases, they contribute very little to the world.

Is this really an enviable way to live?

But *you* are **a rechargeable battery**, capable of change. You are capable of building foundations that are the pillars of lasting happiness. And thus, you possess infinite future possibilities in finding love, success, and fulfillment.

You may have been robbed *temporarily*, simply because you didn't know these people existed. No matter how shattered you may be, you will recover – you just don't know it yet.

You can overcome the temporary setback by taking positive action and moving forward.

It doesn't matter how pretty the presentation is. The core of the psychopath's ethos is a fraud. Once you get over the emotional aspect of the situation and see their core for what they truly are, they are losers and poor investments **for you**.

Don't be jealous of their life together. Psychopathic individuals are masters of impression management. They live a double life – a false, confident personality on the outside and an internal ugliness that's bound to come out sooner or later, through the illusions. Photographs and constant Facebook updates are just that, illusions. How do we know that's really their reality? It generally takes two healthy people to have a happy relationship. One toxic person and a new, naive source of supply are not the ingredients that bode well for long-term happiness.

The glamorous illusion and the sad reality can be seen in the example of Manohara Odella Pinot, a 17-year-old Indonesian model who married a Malaysian prince and became a royal princess. In magazines, on TV, and from afar, she seemed extremely lucky, achieving the pinnacle of what every girl in Indonesia aspired to. But after Ms. Pinot escaped, she alleged that she was treated like an animal and a sex slave, her husband's property. She claimed that she had been isolated in a foreign country with no friends or relatives and injected with tranquilizers by guards and doctors to be kept in the bedroom. Under threats of beatings, she was forced to maintain a happy facade at public events. *"After the first minute of the marriage solemnization, he quickly changed into a psychopath. It was true that he wanted to separate me from my mother,"* Manohara said.

Be glad for freedom. You have time, the most precious resource, free from bondage and unperturbed by toxic individuals. Don't let it go to waste.

Now the question is, what will you do with your freedom, precious time, and new-found inner truth?

How to Avoid Facebook, Social Media, and All Reminders

During the healing stage, to protect your own well-being, make an absolute rule not to look at that person's or their friends' Facebook pages. This is for two reasons:

1. For a psychopath, appearance is **everything**. **That's all they have.** It's almost an instinctual behavior to put on a front of success and happiness, no matter what the truth is. No matter what happens, their Facebook and social media profiles will always be plastered with illusions – looking happy, successful, even if they are heading to prison tomorrow. Once you understand the fakeness, it's comical, even pitiful. The sneak peek will only serve to make you feel bad about your situation or to trigger bad memories.

2. Once a psychopath is done with you and has moved on to a new target, they engineer the job interview process we looked at all over again, with a brand-new persona designed to work a new target. Consequently, their Facebook identity may all of sudden become an opposite identity. Their interests, religion, and personality may change completely, and pictures of their new performance will be everywhere. You don't need to be involved or be reminded of any of these crazy antics.

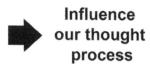

Daily images we see or things we hear → **Influence our thought process** → **Trigger our emotions**

It's best to destroy all physical traces of their existence. Block all calls, texts, emails; get rid of all physical reminders of them; and avoid accidental meetings and places that remind you of them. Implement tactics so that they don't have the means to keep tabs on your life.

How to Establish NCEA (No Contact Ever Again) Strategically

Establishing NCEA in tiered steps or stages works the best. Psychologically, sometimes you need to trick yourself to make sure you adhere to what's best for you.

1. Make a promise to yourself not to establish contact until you are completely over that person, and they have no further power to affect any of your emotions. Think of this as something temporary you must do, not permanent. It may take a couple of months or even years **but give yourself the gift to heal unperturbed in the best environment possible.** Then take action to focus 100% on your healing and your happiness. Do not attempt any contact until you arrive at a point where your emotions toward the psychopath become complete indifference.

2. Sooner or later, you will be over it. When you are sufficiently distanced from the excruciating dramas, then it's the time to be rational about things. If the urge comes up, review the lists recommended later on and make a rational cost/benefit analysis to see whether the risks are worth it.

3. You will likely find the longer you stay away from the toxicity, the more you can allow the sunshine back into your life again; your heart will feel warm, glowing, and radiant once again. When you eventually notice this, be sure to record this transition or moment in time. This will help you remember to stay centered and never to allow external influences to destroy your hard-won serenity and happiness.

How to Master and Conquer Fear

When we talk about fear, we must differentiate between two kinds. Most mainstream guides on conquering 'fear' are about the fear of failure or phobias, with the end goal being personal growth and positive, uplifting outcomes.

The type of fear with a psychopath and the type of fear I am talking about is a paralyzing one.

This is a cowering in your closet, quivering all over your body, fearing for your life type of fear. It's a debilitating fear that *completely paralyzes you* from inside out. This is your mind and body responding in red emergency alert – your fight and flight mechanism shaken. Only those who have been through similar experiences can possibly understand.

Some of the symptoms include:

- Disturbed mind
- Panic attacks
- Chronic anxiety
- Instant physical and mental paralysis with any reminders of the psychopath

In my experience, there are only three things that can counteract this severely debilitating state.

First, you must get to a safe environment where you can heal.

After an encounter with a psychopath, your sense of safety has been shattered. Your psyche endured deep damage, as if an intruder cracked into your deepest core and massacred all your invisible protections. You feel raw, vulnerable, and fearful towards the world and *everything external.*

It will take time to heal this invisible crack in your psyche. In a safe environment though, fearful symptoms generally last about one year before they dissipate, and your body natural-ly rebuilds its safety mechanisms. During this healing stage, make sure you get to a safe, cozy environment that supplies what your psyche needs to heal the damage naturally.

Second, you must channel all your emotions into a controlled counter-offense.

What do I mean by this? It means that while you can't con-trol the psychopath's behavior, there are many things you can do to strengthen and protect yourself.

The word 'controlled' means a productive direction of your fearful energy. The word 'counter-offense' means action and doing everything in your power to strengthen yourself – from a paralyzing mess into focused, full-on attack mode.

I want you to visualize a life or death confrontation when push comes to shove. At that moment when your life is in danger, what will you do to survive? How will you defend yourself?

Then I want you to channel all your fear and all your anger into hard, practical actions to master defense, should this need *ever*, and I mean *ever*, arise.

This means:

- Acquire a firearms license and learn to shoot for self-defense

- Take a self-defense class for physical combat

- Master self-defense on all fronts you can think of (e.g. home surveillance)

- Act aggressively to protect yourself

The keyword here is **Action**. In my experience, only action, aggression and preparation can counteract this paralyzing, debilitating fear.

Again, I am not talking about hurting the psychopath or breaking the law. I am talking about aggressive defense and self-strengthening, *for you*. In extreme circumstances, you have got to turn on an inner ruthlessness when you need it to survive and pause it when you don't.

This is the only way to take your power back. The more you act, the more you practice and prepare, the more this fear will dissipate. And I promise you, the stronger you will feel.

Lastly, you need to learn psychological mindfulness.

A good resource is the book *The Power of Now* by Eckhart Tolle. The concepts are deep, and the techniques take practice, but they are rewarding.

In summary, the book says that, essentially, all suffering is caused by attachment to the past, and apprehension for the future. But the past is only a memory and the future a mirage. Both are an illusion of time, they are not *real*. Yet they cause all the negativity and suffering we experience. The only real moment is the now.

To combat the paralyzing fear, learn to be present in the now. Being in the now frees you from your anxious mind and lets go of all the negative baggage associated with the past and future. It completely shifts your sensory perceptions to a deep, present awareness; and with it ends anxiety, stress, panic attacks, etc. One becomes calm and your thoughts become slowed down and controlled, and you are more prepared to deal with whatever life throws at you.

How to Adopt the Standard of a Blissful Constant

"Before you diagnose yourself with depression or low self-esteem, first make sure that you are not, in fact, just surrounding yourself with assholes."

– William Gibson

This original idea was adapted from the book *Psychopath Free* by Jackson MacKenzie.[1] It aims at having a solid baseline through ties with a person who inspires feelings of heartwarming love, trust, and reliability. That private baseline can be used as a measurement to weed out negative people from your life.

Steps to Obtaining a Constant

1. Think of someone you love and who loves you. It can be family, friends, a deceased someone, or even a pet. The important thing is that the person or entity you pick as a constant should always make you feel safe and peaceful. They should possess qualities you admire, such as kindness and compassion.

2. Now ponder three questions for yourself:

   - How do you feel round your constant?

   - Does your constant make you feel anxious, jealous, insecure, and other bad emotions?

   - What is the difference between your constant and people who make you feel awful or unbalanced?

3. When you meet people with negative energy, recall the positivity your constant brings out in you.

   - Remember that you are not crazy. After all, you are totally normal around your constant. Not only that, you are the best version of yourself.

   - Understand that good people make you feel good, and bad people make you feel bad.

4. Decide whether you still want to be around people who bring out negativity in you.

How to Embrace the Power of Lists

This exercise involves structuring your thoughts around what is often an emotionally loaded, painful topic through writing a series of tailored lists. It is powerful and incredibly therapeutic.

First, it utilizes how our brain naturally converts information. When you write things down, your brain automatically translates the emotionally incomprehensible to become logically comprehensible. However, when you verbalize the past in continuing 'to talk about it', you may relive the trauma and emotional turmoil all over again. Detaching and comprehending is one of the first paths to healing.

Second, these lists take your mind off a toxic past and focus you on to a new world of unlimited, positive potentials. You will be able to embrace new ideas and endeavors that are now open to you. The best part is that you gain an instant freedom and feeling of hope, simply by reviewing your lists again and again.

The first batch of lists focus on rationality so as to separate reality from illusion and see the truth with clarity.

1. Make a list of everyone you know personally that you really admire – people of generosity, genuineness, strong moral compass, substance, and courage; people who are doing amazing, admirable, great things in life. They might be family members, friends, old bosses, or co-workers. Now compare your real-life heroes to the psychopath in terms of character, actions, life goals, and how they make others feel. Would your real-life heroes do what the psychopath did?

This comparison tactic really does work and is quite powerful. The psychopath compared you against everyone else. Isn't it time to compare them against your heroes?

When you take your mind away from their illusory persona and the emotions of the situation, the psychopath comes up as, well, just pretty much scum – disgusting and kind of worthless in comparison to people you respect.

This is how you direct your thoughts from here on out, not through the manufactured persona that created artificial desirability.

2. Write down all the reasons that you miss the psychopath.

3. Write down all the reasons that it is better that he or she is out of your life.

The next batch puts the focus back on you – on your happiness and self-improvement. It gives you something bigger to focus on. Your life is worth so much more. It is much bigger than one toxic and temporary situation.

1. Write down what you want to achieve, in terms of short-term, medium-term, and long-term goals.

2. Write down everything you are passionate about.

3. Write down everything that you are grateful for. For example, family, friends, personal skillsets, past achievements, present enjoyments, and so on. During our down time, we don't see the gifts we already have that make our lives wonderful, and the qualities that no one can ever, permanently take away.

4. What do you love about yourself? Celebrate your good qualities.

Now the last two lists are inner reflections. They ensure the lessons learned stay with you for the rest of your life. You may need some time and introspection before you are ready. But once you have the lists down, you will always have a precious reminder to safeguard your personal well-being, values, and long-term happiness.

1. Write a list of what attracted you to the psychopath in the first place. Was it looks? Promises of true love? Attention? A need to be needed? A need to feel approval? A desire to reform someone? A fear of being alone? Use this list to understand what is inside of you that made you vulnerable to them in the first place. Get to know yourself so you won't be blindsided again by a future invader that provides little value.

2. Lastly, make a list of priority qualities **before** you look for someone new to date. Focus on internal qualities that are important to you. But keep this list to yourself and don't advertise what you are looking for, as a predator can quickly assume that persona.

Now review these lists weekly, or whenever you think of the psychopath. Eventually, your brain will automatically adjust 180 degrees. You will be happy they are out of your life, while focusing on the thing that truly matters – you.

Chapter 7. Final Thoughts

"You do not need to be loved, not at the cost of yourself. The single relationship that is truly central and crucial in life is the relationship to the self."

– Jo Courdert

"The depth and strength of a human character are defined by its moral reserves. People reveal themselves completely only when they are thrown out of the customary conditions of their life, for only then do they have to fall back on their reserves."

– Leon Trotsky

The most important thing is to build yourself up. The main thing that will ban all future psychopaths, sociopaths, and narcissists from your life is cultivating a healthy self-esteem. To achieve this, you need a combination of hard tools and soft tools. The hard tools are conscious rules made by you, derived from logic and individual experience. The soft tools are powerful self-care practices that works on the unconscious level to build internal strength.

I am including a sample to get you started.

A Sample of My Rules

Through personal experience, I have set up certain rules and boundaries I now live by. And I encourage you to develop and write down your own list of rules.

For empaths like us to grow and stand strong in our own energy, we need to actively police our lives for toxins and polluting influences.

As individuals, we are each responsible for our own worlds – what interactions we accept and who is allowed to be there. **It's time to take back active control**, instead of blindly and complaisantly accepting each circumstance or person that happens to float our way.

Each of us has different needs depending on our own set of values, personalities, and what we ultimately need to maximize our happiness and well-being.

My rules may seem strict. However, I have too much experience with unscrupulous individuals to relax my rules at the drop of a hat. I value my sanity a great deal. Certainly, the rules are not lifetime absolutes; they remain subject to amendment as life progresses. They simply represent the current stage of my consciousness and development.

Below are my personal rules. What are yours?

1. **Lost trust: No contact ever again unless formally necessary.**

   If anyone breaks my trust in a major way, they are out of my personal circle ASAP. Life is unpredictable enough on its own. Adding people with questionable motives, character, or intentions into my life is self-defeating. To me, it means I am actively allowing future problems to manifest and grow. It's much easier to cut them out now than allowing that person to take advantage or manipulate future situations, potentially at a high cost to myself or those close to me. Prevention is less costly, so I cut them out ruthlessly.

What is 'formally necessary' contact? This means contact which is necessary or unavoidable due to business, law, social circles, or etiquette. In those cases, I will enforce boundaries and maintain a conservative, formal distance. For me, it's not obligatory to close that gap and no one should feel entitled to ask it.

2. Habitual manipulation: Out of my personal life immediately.

While many people may use elements of manipulation to a certain degree, I never trust a habitual manipulator. If I realize someone uses manipulation consistently as their main interpersonal tool and interactive style, and there is a low likelihood they will ever change, they are out of my personal life immediately.

Why? Because I just don't have time for the exhausting, tit-for-tat mental games required to constantly psychoanalyze someone's motives or covert agendas. I prefer being around people with whom I am comfortable and can relax. I also prefer to focus and direct my mental energy toward winning *constructive* battles, not shielding against covert aggression or mind games.

Here is the equation I mentally operate by:

Manipulation = hiding their true intentions to gain and fight for control under a guise = deception = no trust = no contact unless formally necessary.

3. **Full background check on anyone significant that comes into my life. This can be in romance, a new best friend, business partnerships, full-time employment, and even for landlords.**

This step is a small preventative investment to safeguard a great deal later on. I execute this as due process no matter how highly recommended they come or how charming the outward presentation is.

Specifics I look for include:

- Restraining orders.

- Assault and battery. Have they any – and I mean **any** – prior charges for domestic battery.

- Any misdemeanors, law breaking, jail or prison time.

- Previous marriages, kids, spouses in different states.

- Current or previous alias used. Information under both birth name and alias.

- If a landlord, problems with previous tenants at small claims and county courts.

- If a landlord, tenant ratings and feedback on social media sites.

- If military, dishonorable discharges and other records (through the Armed Forces Courts website).

4. **Instead of socializing indiscriminately and desiring everyone to like me, I put my guard up around people who:**

- **Use pity plays to arouse sympathies.** I'm especially suspicious if a person is over, say, age 30 and uses pity plays on those they've only known for a short time. At a certain age, a person has gained enough life experience that you can no longer excuse them on the basis of having an innocent, naive character. They ought also to be socially aware enough to comprehend the social norm of presenting a self-reliant front, regardless of personal insecurities. Consequently, you have to wonder why they are employing this tactic.

- **Flatters excessively.** It can be sycophantic at best, and at worst evidence of a secret, manipulative agenda.

- **Has weird eyes or gives weird stares; uses uninterrupted eye contact to seduce, put someone in a hypnotizing trance, or to intimidate; or has a shifty-eyed, shady look.** In my personal experience, the eyes really are the windows to the soul. Sometimes people really aren't aware of how they look, but when combined with the other behaviors on this list, intense, prolonged, and seductive stares flag up my suspicions.

- **Displays high levels of testosterone with aggressive, pushy behavior.** These people may not be psychopaths, sociopaths, or narcissists per se, but they are often draining and exhausting. Typically, they constitute ticking time bombs for unnecessary drama.

- **Pushes boundaries, is intrusive, and becomes too familiar during initial meetings.** This is especially true in inappropriate social situations. For example, volunteering excessive personal and private information without being asked in professional settings, such as a job interview. I have to wonder why someone would volunteer unsolicited information in settings that clearly don't call for it. Are they trying to control or maneuver others' perceptions of their image? If so, why do they need to?

5. Develop and practice a 'stone face' to be used in certain life situations.

I practice an unsmiling, to-the-point facade with certain people and within certain situations. Gone are the days where I am smiling and showing my intrinsic kindness for everyone to see. It simply isn't practical in real life. There are people and situations that necessitate different treatment. Many such are looking for openings to worm their way in for personal benefit without having others' best interests at heart.

My stone face is deliberate and calculated, accompanied with strong, confident body language, and often used with variants of simple rebuttals that put up a wall, such as *'Why do you ask? Why do you want to know? What exactly is your motive for asking?'* Or the much more explicit, *'I believe private information should remain private, and I would appreciate it if you can respect those boundaries'.* In those situations, I assert my needs and hint at the possibility of confrontation, while staying below the level of overt rudeness or conflict. I do so without feeling guilt or worrying about being nice or polite.

6. Immediately respond to any boundary violations, either with calm actions to restore dignity or by putting a stop to it with stricter boundaries.

Boundary pushing isn't only regulated to unscrupulous people. It can also be a result of cultural norms and ingrained attitudes of behavior. In these situations, the person needs to be told in a polite, neutral manner the first time it happens that their actions are not appropriate. Otherwise, lacking cues to stop, they will push an inch to a mile.

In the past, I was often slow to take action, waiting until something grew to bigger proportions. This inaction may have been due to the subtlety of the red flag behavior, as well as my general preference for peace rather than conflict.

I have since learned that silence equals consent and compliance in the perpetrator's eyes. Second, silence in the face of something that bothers you only allows anger to build. When continuously bottled up, this anger may lead to inappropriate release.

What I do now is respond as soon as it happens. This is different from reacting impulsively. Reacting impulsively to what someone did to you may escalate things into conflict and give the other party power. Instead, I respond in ways that preserve my boundaries, dignity, and best interests; sometimes with words and actions, and other times only with actions. In using words, I'm to-the-point, stating my position calmly and clearly, without making accusations or encouraging conflict. Responding does not acknowledge anyone's power over or ability to affect me; it only acknowledges my position on the matter.

7. **If the person exhibits characteristics of a full-on sociopath or psychopath, I stay the hell away.**

This is what I do no matter how I feel emotionally. The potential consequences are wasting typically 12 to 24 months in emotional recovery and other types of recuperation. I can't afford that in my life.

8. **Observe if the person has any real friends. If the answer is no, there is *always* a reason why.**

I view this rule as a shortcut to discover character-disordered individuals. For some reason, every single person I have ever met who had no real friends (no warm and close bonds), even though they lived in a place long enough to generate friendships, had something really wrong with their personality or character. Associating with them up close, or over the longer term, always produced negative outcomes.

For example, I have encountered questionable landlords who play a stream of tenants for deposit money and sport. I've met expatriates who form relationships and friendships with the underlying motive of obtaining a green card or US citizenship. These are covertly manipulative and needy relationships, instead of open or transparent ones.

I've since mentally established a logical spectrum – at best, friendless individuals may be socially inappropriate and insecure; in the middle spectrum, they may be draining, emotional vampires; at worst, they are full-on sociopaths and psychopaths. Unfortunately, none of the three work for my needs.

9. Reserve trust until it is earned.

Based on consistency between words, actions, and a period of observation of how the person acts in the little moments, you can choose to give or withhold trust.

10. Always ask about the person's reputation among people who know them or have knowledge of them. If someone has a bad reputation with shady elements, I don't engage with them any further or closer.

While it's important to get your own impression and vibes from a person, times come when we all have blind spots. I realized sometimes I tend to idealize people with my own filter bias. Consequently, it really helps to have second opinions from trustworthy sources, in order to contrast with, validate, and reflect with my own assessment and the subtle cues I may have ignored. I find a lot of value in privately hearing others' honest opinions. Good venues are:

- People who are outside the main individual's circle of influence. These people are unbiased and can offer valuable insight.

- People who have a prior history with the person or know them in a different capacity than the facet shown to me. Even very short-term interactions can offer insight.

- The grapevine – news of someone's reputation can be a valuable source of supplemental information.

All this weaves a cohesive picture of pattern and personality, which can be value added to make informed decisions. Frequently one's past behaviors foreshadow future ones.

Certainly, there are people whose nice personas are entirely different from their private lives. Even those people do not fool everyone. Doing my own research allows me to see beyond.

Positive Mantras to Build Internal Strength

Below are the mantras for a newer and stronger you. When you are ready, pick whichever mantra resonates and make those promises to yourself.

- I promise myself that no one will ever take advantage of me again.

- I promise myself that I will no longer be naive, blind, and sleepy to the existence of the secretly poisonous. I will learn to spot them and erect firm boundaries to keep them out.

- I promise myself that I will only surround myself **with people who bring out the best in me**. My peace of mind, serenity, health, and emotional well-being are hard won. I understand that **letting in even one toxic person** can destroy my dreams, my goals, my confidence, and everything I have worked extremely hard to build. **I care about my life and my goals too much to let that ever happen again.**

- I promise myself that I will differentiate between **words and actions**.

- I promise myself that I will love myself, my perceived flaws, insincerities, everything. I know that compared to those that are nothing but utter emptiness, **I am actually pretty awesome!** I would rather be a light-filled entity with heart, warmth, humanity, love, and conscience **and** natural human flaws than a hollow vessel – no matter how flashy or pretty the exterior cover-up.

- I promise myself that I will no longer waste my precious gifts of love, attention, resources, sympathy, and joy on those who are undeserving. I will only share these gifts with those who are truly deserving and are deemed worthy in my life.

- **I promise myself that no matter what tortuous emotions I feel temporarily, I value my health, sanity, and well-being above all. I will not establish any contact until I am completely over this person and they no longer have any power to affect me.**

- I promise myself that **I will no longer blindly trust appearances**. I will question authority, titles, the surface image, and the role people assume in society. I will let time and people's actions reveal their core character and integrity.

- I promise myself that if I feel drained or unhappy with a situation, environment, or person, **I will take the necessary action to change the situation and move my life forward.** I have the power to make that choice in an intelligent and strategic manner, even if it means cutting the cause of that drain out of my life permanently, and without regret.

Remember, a promise is a promise.

About the Author

Zane Alexander woke up one day tired of being manipulated, hurt, and deceived by pathological personalities.

So, she set to work and read every book and resource she could find on the subject and studied in every area she could get her hands on. After three years, she finished the best-selling guide book on psychopaths, sociopaths, and narcissists.

As a first-hand survivor with real life experience, Zane goes beyond the clinical to real-world solutions. She will teach you everything you need to know to deal with these types in the real world.

The game is **substance** and **usefulness**.

You can find her original articles at **SociopathFree.com**

Get notified of all her upcoming articles, courses, books, and videos by signing up at **SociopathFree.com/Signup**

Chapter Notes

A Key Reminder of the NCEA (No Contact Ever Again) Social Rule

1. Hare, Robert D. and Neumann, Craig S. (2008). "Psychopathy as a Clinical and Empirical Construct". *Annual Review of Clinical Psychology*. 4 (1): 217–46.

Chapter 1. The 80/20 Basics

1. Stout, Martha. *The Sociopath Next Door: The Ruthless Versus the Rest of Us* (New York: Broadway Books, 2005), 9.

2. Hare, Robert D. (2003). *Manual for the Revised Psychopathy Checklist (2nd ed.)*. Toronto, ON, Canada: Multi-Health Systems.

3. Stout, Martha. *The Sociopath Next Door: The Ruthless Versus the Rest of Us* (New York: Broadway Books, 2005), 109.

4. Sheridan, Thomas. *Puzzling People: The Labyrinth of the Psychopath* (Velluminous Press, 2011), 67–70.

5. Hare, Robert D. *Without Conscience: The Disturbing World of the Psychopaths Among Us* (New York: Guilford Press, 1999), 195–200. Scientifically, this was first noted by Hare in his publication.

Chapter 2. Methods of Operation

1. Hare, Robert D. *Without Conscience: The Disturbing World of the Psychopaths Among Us* (New York: Guilford Press, 1999), 81. This book cited Robert Linder's book *Rebel Without a Cause* (see below) and built upon the points made.

2. Lindner, Robert. *Rebel Without a Cause* (New York: Grune and Stratton, 1944).

3. Babiak, Paul, and Hare, Robert D. *Snakes in Suits: When Psychopaths Go to Work* (New York: Regan Books, 2006).

4. Babiak, Paul, and Hare, Robert D. *Snakes in Suits: When Psychopaths Go to Work* (New York: Regan Books, 2006), 128–131.

5. Babiak, Paul, and Hare, Robert D. *Snakes in Suits: When Psychopaths Go to Work* (New York: Regan Books, 2006), 42–58.

6. Babiak, Paul, and Hare, Robert D. *Snakes in Suits: When Psychopaths Go to Work* (New York: Regan Books, 2006), 111–141. In the book, Babiak and Hare called it Pawns, Patrons, and Patsies. Instead of the word 'Patsies', the concept is simplified here to 'useless' to better describe the psychopath mindset.

7. Babiak, Paul, and Hare, Robert D. *Snakes in Suits: When Psychopaths Go to Work* (New York: Regan Books, 2006), 129–130.

8. Babiak, Paul, and Hare, Robert D. *Snakes in Suits: When Psychopaths Go to Work* (New York: Regan Books, 2006), 285–286.

9. Babiak, Paul, and Hare, Robert D. *Snakes in Suits: When Psychopaths Go to Work* (New York: Regan Books, 2006), 299–300.

10. Al Mualla, Saoud. *How to Manipulate the Manipulator: A Guide to Winning the War Against Deceitful Individuals* (Central Milton Keynes: AuthorHouse, 2009), 66.

Chapter 3. How to Defend Yourself Once and For All

1. Stout, Martha. *The Sociopath Next Door: The Ruthless Versus the Rest of Us.* (New York: Broadway Books, 2005), 156.

2. Simon, George, K. *In Sheep's Clothing: Understanding and Dealing with Manipulative People.* New York: (Parkhurst Brothers, 2010), 155–157.

3. Positivagirl. "Sociopath – How to Get Even with One." www.datingasociopath.com, web blog post. Dating a Sociopath, March 8, 2013. Web. 2016.

Chapter 4. The Female Psychopath

1. Sheridan, Thomas. *Puzzling People: The Labyrinth of the Psychopath* (Velluminous Press, 2011), 39, 70–72, 165–166.

Chapter 6. How to Get Over Them in Real Life

1. MacKenzie, Jackson. *Psychopath Free (Expanded Edition): Recovering from Emotionally Abusive Relationships with Narcissists, Sociopaths, and Other Toxic People* (New York: Berkley Books, 2015), 12–18, Kindle.

Selected Reading

I recommend all the books and blogs cited in the chapter notes, as those are genre classics. In addition, here is a short list of carefully curated and selected reading material that will give you a more well-rounded perspective in the genre:

Splitting: Protecting Yourself While Divorcing Someone with Borderline or Narcissistic Personality Disorder
by Bill Eddy and Randi Kreger (best legal guide on market)

The Gift of Fear: Survival Signals That Protect Us from Violence
by Gavin De Becker

How to Spot a Dangerous Man Before You Get Involved
by Sandra Brown

Who's Pulling Your Strings? How to Break the Cycle of Manipulation and Regain Control of Your Life
by Harriet Braiker

A Dance with the Devil: A True Story of Marriage to a Psychopath
by Barbara Bentley

One Last Thing

If you loved this guide, there are three things you can do to spread the word:

#1: You can write a review

Your support really does make a difference. Every review counts! If you found anything of value in the book, then please leave a review.

What did you think of this book? Did you like this book? Did this book help you? What are the top three things you will implement going forward?

#2: You can spread the wisdom

This guide is written with the aim to help empathetic individuals navigate this hidden terrain with practicality and clarity. Send it to those for whom it can be of practical use and help. Let them know the existence of this body of research and the long-term value it can provide to their life.

Some suggested ideas are:

- Email it to private survivor circles.

- Mention it on psychopath and sociopath forums that are aimed to help targets and victims.

- Private message those who may be going through the same devastation.

Once you understand the existence of these people (and see the deeper glimpses underneath our everyday superficialities), you are removed from the rest of society that do not. Most people will not be ready for it, as many have never met one. Understand that there may be nothing you can do to change their mind. Only a life experience will make them ready. The only thing you can do is be there for those you care about. Give them the handbook only when they are ready, and love and support them when they need it.

#3: Give a copy to somebody else

May I ask you for a favor?

If this book helped you, if you highlighted parts of it, if you feel empowered by the message, or if it transformed your inner life in any way, I am hoping you will do something for me. Give a copy to somebody else. Ask them to read it. Let them know the existence of the hidden terrain and what they must do to remain sane, healthy, and happy.

Those with a conscience need a solid defense system. Spread the word.

Thank you.

Zane

58092702R00120

Made in the USA
Columbia, SC
17 May 2019